THE PUBLIC LIBRARIES
OF GREATER LONDON
A pictorial history 1856-1914

Below: The City of Westminster Literary, Scientific and Mechanics' Institution was situated in Great Smith Street. A view by T. H. Shepherd. The lettering across the façade of the building has a robust disregard for accuracy. The Institution became the first public library in London and this view should be compared with that at the start of the section on Adapted Premises (page 23). As T. H. Shepherd was active between 1817 and 1840, this view was presumably done for the opening of the Institution in 1837

Alan W. Ball

The Public Libraries of Greater London

A pictorial history 1856-1914

LIBRARY ASSOCIATION
LONDON AND HOME COUNTIES BRANCH
1977

TO

TOM BARNARD and ERIC WINTER

In memory of the many happy and
often hilarious hours spent in their company,
when dealing with the business affairs of
the London and Home Counties Branch
of the Library Association

Above: Memorial tablets placed in Edmonton Central Library
by John Passmore Edwards in 1898. They were executed
by George Frampton. (See page 36 for further
details of this donation.)

© Alan W. Ball, 1977

All rights reserved. No part of this publication may be reproduced, stored in a retrieval system or transmitted, in any form or by any means, electronic, mechanical, photocopying, recording or otherwise without prior permission of the London and Home Counties Branch of the Library Association

ISBN 0 902119 17 6 (Cloth)
ISBN 0 902119 18 4 (Paperback)

Printed and bound in England by
STAPLES PRINTERS LIMITED
at The Stanhope Press, Rochester, Kent

CONTENTS

	Page
General Introduction	6
Subscription Libraries and Mechanics' Institutes	7
For and Against the Acts	11
Adapted Premises	23
Benefactors	32
Stone Laying Ceremonies	36
Opening Ceremonies	45
Architects and Library Buildings	57
Living on the Job	72
Furniture and Fittings	73
Lighting, Heating and Ventilation	77
Lending Libraries	78
Reference Libraries	81
Children's Libraries	84
Newsrooms	85
Lecture Halls	88
Cataloguing Departments, Catalogues and Classification Schemes	89
Books and Readers	91
Chiefs	94
Library Staff	97
Caretakers and Cleaners	100
Committees and Finance	102
Transport	106
The Shadow of War	106
Acknowledgements	106
Suggestions for Further Reading	107
Index of Buildings Illustrated	108

General Introduction

This work has been produced as a contribution to the celebrations marking the centenary of the foundation of the Library Association in 1877. A wealth of pictorial material exists in London public libraries, and it seemed to the Committee of the London and Home Counties Branch, an opportune moment to make this available to a wider audience. It was quite clear from the outset, that an attempt to cover the whole period from the agitation for the first public library in the combined parishes of St. Margaret and St. John, Westminster, in 1856 up to the present, would have been extremely superficial. It was therefore decided to limit the present volume to the period from 1856 to the outbreak of the first world war.

Instead of trying to produce a work filled with detailed cross-references, reliance has been placed on the Suggestions for Further Reading on page 107, to carry the reader from the text to source material. The photographs and other illustrations speak for themselves and the linking narrative and captions merely serve as the minimum background information to make them intelligible.

It is as well at the outset to define the area to be covered. London consists of a large number of villages, that have been swallowed up by the urban sprawl, which has advanced steadily ever since building started outside the square mile of the original City. It is not usually appreciated by those from other parts of the country or abroad, how fierce is the tribal attachment of Londoners to their own particular village. Confusion about purely local government boundaries is widespread and loyalty is given to the village first and the municipality a long way behind.

As in rural communities, London villagers have often not heard of other villages at a distance, much less visited them. If you stopped people at random in the streets of Hither Green and asked them to tell you exactly where Stroud Green, Sands End, Cubitt Town, Child's Hill, Brondesbury, The Borough and Stamford Brook are situated, you would be very fortunate to receive an exact answer. If you then asked in which of the London Boroughs created in 1965, these places are to be found, you would almost certainly be given a large number of incorrect replies.

Public libraries were being set up during the period up to 1914 throughout what is now the area of the Greater London Council and the City of London, except for the present London Boroughs of Barnet, Harrow, Havering, Hillingdon and Sutton. Therefore I felt that a much more rounded picture would be created by the inclusion of material from as many library authorities as possible and, accordingly, have not concentrated exclusively on the vestries and Metropolitan Boroughs, which succeeded them, within what is perhaps now best described as the area of the Inner London Education Authority, but also turned my attention to the surrounding districts and called this whole area simply Greater London.

It can of course be argued that this is illogical, as these outer districts were situated at that time in the counties of Middlesex, Surrey, Essex and Kent. This is perfectly correct, but as I have been at pains to point out earlier, local government boundaries change while communities remain. As a native of a London village, I feel sure nobody will begrudge me the right to define exactly what I mean by the place where I was born, especially as this concept of Greater London was adopted as long ago as 1829 for police purposes and 1875 by the Registrar General for vital statistics.

One other complication remains. When dealing with general matters in the main text, I have relied on the currently familiar nomenclature of library committees, councillors, aldermen and mayors. In producing captions for photographs, I have been more specific and mentioned library commissioners and vestrymen in the inner areas, if the date precedes the formation of the Metropolitan Boroughs in 1899. However, I have for the most part tried to skirt delicately round the edge of the morass, which is London municipal history. For those who wish to pursue this fascinating and Byzantine field of study further, I have made suggestions on pages 107 and 108.

Finally, all geographical details about buildings refer to the local authority name at the time when they were constructed, as I feel that readers ought to be persuaded into a little detective work. If they wish to translate the situation into the post 1965 setting of the present London Boroughs, they should consult the index on page 108.

Subscription Libraries and Mechanics' Institutes

Before the first public libraries were set up as a result of the original Acts from 1850 onwards, people wishing to borrow books had to do so from subscription libraries or mechanics' institutes. Illustrations of the latter in the London area are very difficult to find, although a certain number of the former appeared in periodicals.

Subscription libraries continued of course until well after the second world war, sometimes run by local newsagents, but also as highly organised departments of national chain stores such as Boots and W. H. Smith.

The books provided were mostly light fiction, travel and biographies and in marked contrast to those on the shelves of the very small number of scholarly libraries, also charging a subscription. Although the majority of these have perished, the most famous of all, the London Library, still flourishes in spite of the many problems associated with rising costs.

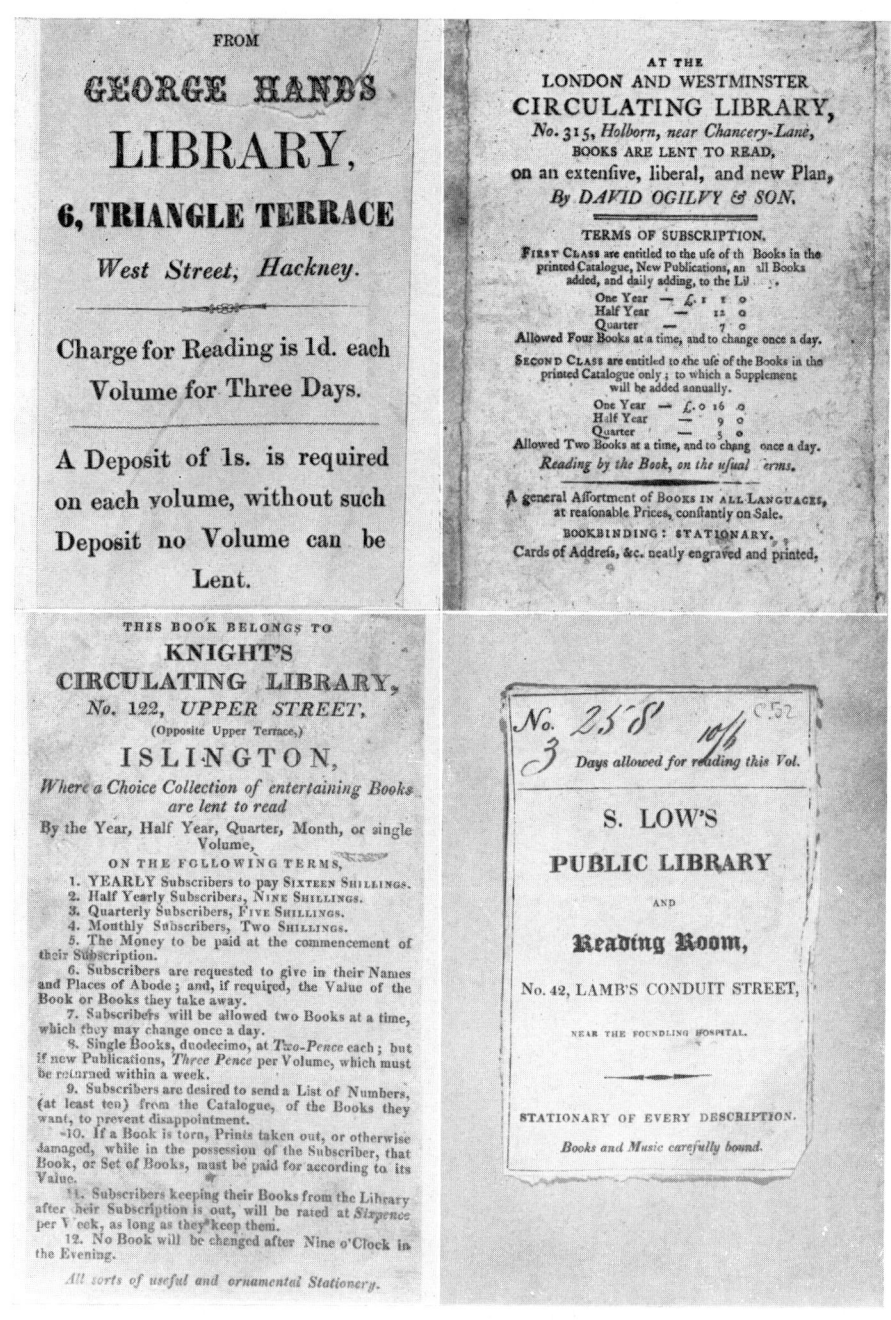

Above: Advertising material with details of charges and subscriptions included in books available from circulating libraries in areas around the City

CITY OF LONDON NEWS ROOMS

We are advocates for the extension of establishments like that of which we give an engraving, for they tend materially to the diffusion of knowledge on the most economical terms. The CITY OF LONDON NEWS ROOMS were established in the memorable year 1851, and may, therefore, be said to date from the opening of the "Great Exhibition." They have succeeded to an extent that could scarcely have been anticipated, and are thronged with readers. One new and very commodious feature is that of placing newspapers on reading-desks, *open*, so that the columns are displayed in full to the eye. The rooms are open from half-past eight o'clock in the morning until half-past nine in the evening, and the admission is only ONE PENNY—the monthly subscription being 2s. 6d.

All the foreign and home journals are taken; and, with a liberality well worthy of being recorded, no extra fee is demanded for consulting files of papers for the past six months. All the extra editions of the daily papers are taken; orders for advertisements are received; a room for committee meetings may be hired; and letters for subscribers are taken in without charge—the cost to non-subscribers being only one halfpenny each. In addition to these many inducements, coffee and refreshments are to be had, and of the best quality too, on very moderate terms. The situation at No. 66, Cheapside, is exceedingly central, and, with the advantages enumerated, we are not surprised at the flourishing condition of this well-ordered establishment.

Above: The City of London News Rooms. One of the forerunners of the public library newsroom. From *The Lady's Newspaper* March 20th, 1852

Above: The Temple of the Muses. This enormous establishment was set up in the late eighteenth century at one of the corners of Finsbury Square and although primarily a bookshop, there was also a subscription library. It encouraged browsing in 'lounging rooms', the staircase to which can be seen on the left of this illustration. The higher you ascended in the building, the older and shabbier the books became. The whole enterprise was destroyed by fire in the middle of the nineteenth century

> Twickenham, March 28. 1844.
>
> NOTICE is hereby given, that a Public MEETING of the Inhabitants of this place will be held at the Magistrate's Room, on Monday the 8th Inst. at 2 o'Clock.
>
> Sir WILLIAM CLAY, Bart. M.P. in the Chair,
>
> to receive a Report from the Provisional Committee which has been formed for the purpose of promoting the Establishment of a
>
> **Public Reading Room & Library,**
>
> with a view to afford increased means of useful Instruction and Rational Amusement to all Classes, and to consider and determine the best means of effecting the same.
>
> *Signed by order of the Provisional Committee,*
>
> E. H. DONNITHORNE, Hon. Secretary.
>
> W. CURTIS, Printer, Twickenham.

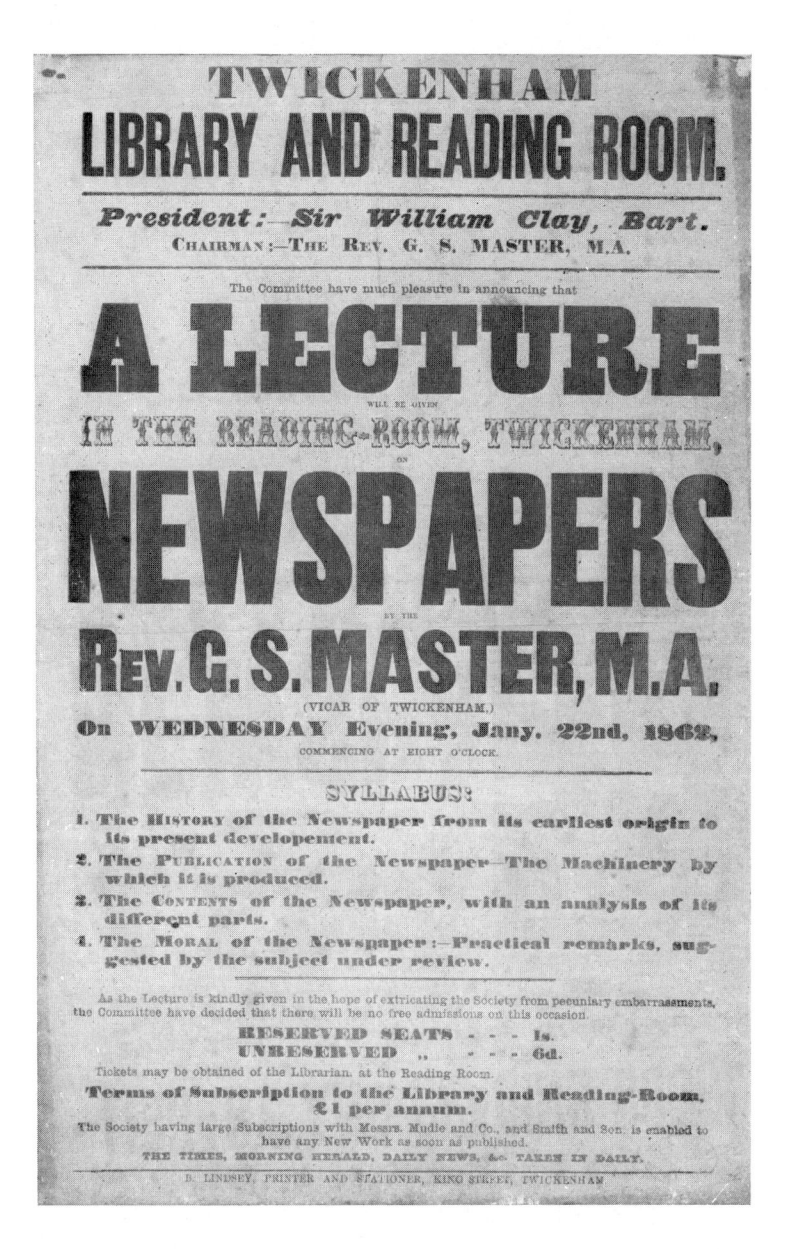

> # TWICKENHAM
> # LIBRARY AND READING ROOM.
>
> President: *Sir William Clay, Bart.*
> CHAIRMAN:—THE REV. G. S. MASTER, M.A.
>
> The Committee have much pleasure in announcing that
>
> # A LECTURE
>
> WILL BE GIVEN
>
> IN THE READING-ROOM, TWICKENHAM,
>
> ON
>
> # NEWSPAPERS
>
> BY THE
>
> # Rev. G. S. MASTER, M.A.
>
> (VICAR OF TWICKENHAM,)
>
> On **WEDNESDAY** Evening, Jany. 22nd, 1862,
>
> COMMENCING AT EIGHT O'CLOCK.
>
> **SYLLABUS:**
>
> 1. The HISTORY of the Newspaper from its earliest origin to its present developement.
> 2. The PUBLICATION of the Newspaper—The Machinery by which it is produced.
> 3. The CONTENTS of the Newspaper, with an analysis of its different parts.
> 4. The MORAL of the Newspaper:—Practical remarks, suggested by the subject under review.
>
> As the Lecture is kindly given in the hope of extricating the Society from pecuniary embarrassments, the Committee have decided that there will be no free admissions on this occasion.
>
> RESERVED SEATS - - - 1s.
> UNRESERVED ,, - - - 6d.
>
> Tickets may be obtained of the Librarian, at the Reading Room.
>
> **Terms of Subscription to the Library and Reading-Room,**
> £1 per annum.
>
> The Society having large Subscriptions with Messrs. Mudie and Co., and Smith and Son, is enabled to have any New Work as soon as published.
>
> THE TIMES, MORNING HERALD, DAILY NEWS, &c. TAKEN IN DAILY.
>
> B. LINDSEY, PRINTER AND STATIONER, KING STREET, TWICKENHAM.

Above: Notice of a public meeting to set up the Twickenham Public Reading Room and Library on March 28th, 1844, and also an advertisement for a public lecture on January 22nd, 1862, clearly intended to extricate the institution from temporary financial difficulties. No minute books or other records exist of this subscription library

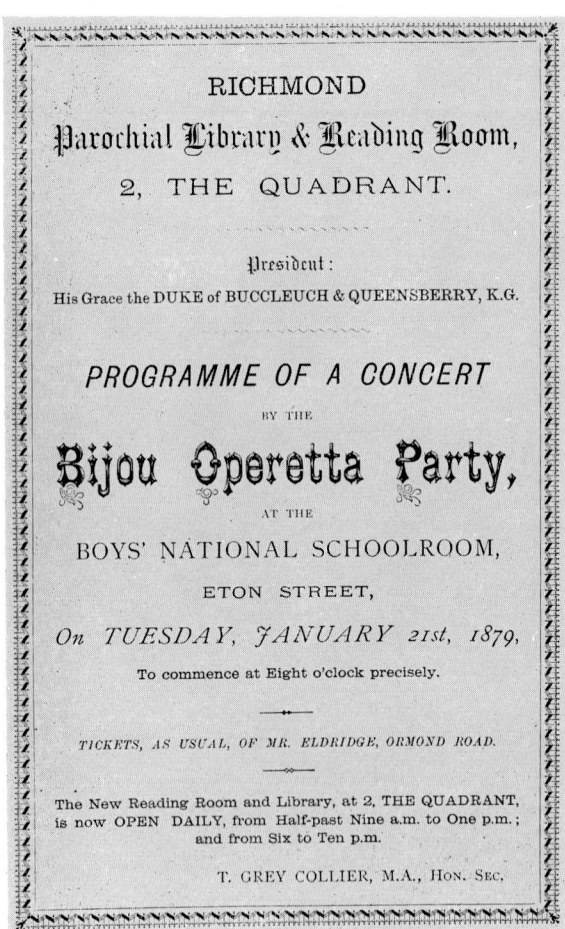
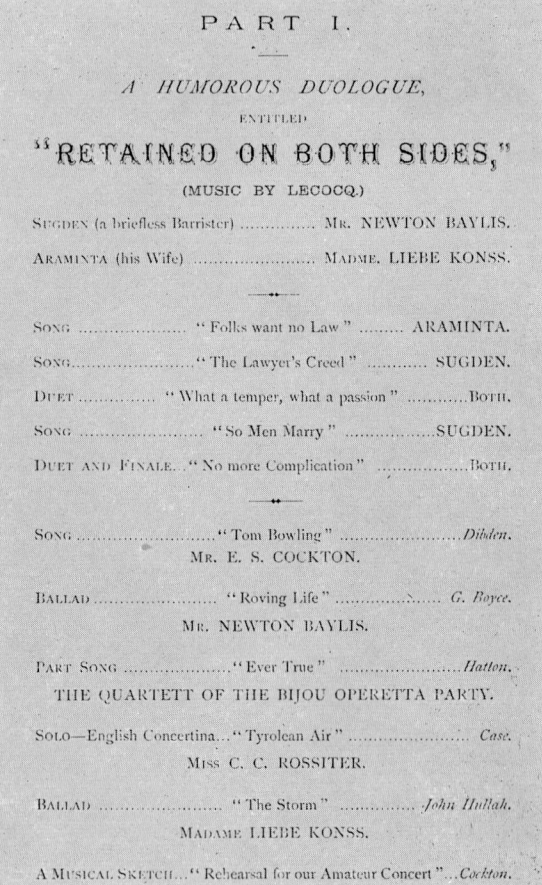

Above: A fund raising concert for the Richmond Parochial Library and Reading Room on January 21st, 1879. The library existed from 1855 to 1888 and its closure was hastened by the opening of the Richmond Public Library in 1881. The Parochial Library originally used a classroom in the National Parochial School and charged an annual subscription, payable in advance, of 6/- for gentlemen and 5/- for ladies. In addition there was a 6d entrance fee. The Librarian was a Mr. Flack, who was paid £6 per annum with free membership. He had two lads as helpers at 6d per week, who came on alternate weeks and had free admission to lectures. The Library was open initially each weekday from 7 pm to 10 pm, and a Mrs. Wheatley was paid £4 per annum for cleaning the room

Below: To paraphrase Voltaire, the Bethnal Green Free Public Library was 'Neither free nor public nor even very much of a library'. Thomas Greenwood in the 1891 edition of his *Public Libraries* was scathing about what he considered its shortcomings. The Public Library Acts were not adopted in Bethnal Green until 1913 and a library not provided until 1922. *Architect:* G. F. Hilcken

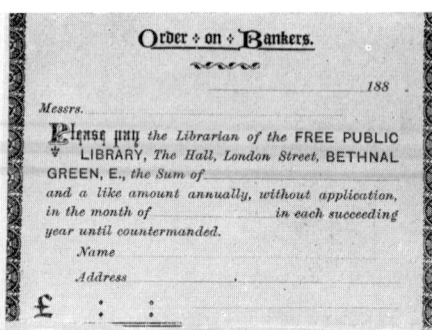

Above: Farm Lodge, Petersham, in April 1901. Petersham had its own village subscription library in Pembroke Lodge from 1874 to 1876 and then in Petersham School from 1876 to 1892. In 1893 it became part of the Richmond Public Library Service. The first room on the ground floor to the left of the photograph was used as a branch reading room. The lady in the doorway is Mrs. A. Colborne, a widow, who was the tenant and caretaker. Few librarians can claim to have carried out their duties in such a delightful building with honeysuckle so much in evidence

For and Against the Acts

Although at this remove of more than a century and a quarter, it would be pleasant to know that the public library service came into being as the result of a widely popular democratic agitation, the reverse is the truth. The original legislation of 1850 was an emasculated mouse of an Act, which only passed the then still largely unreformed House of Commons because it offended nobody.

William Ewart had been forced to agree to a poll of townspeople for the acceptance of the Act and also the albatross of the halfpenny rate limitation, which was hung round its neck. In addition, it was only the amending Act five years later, that actually allowed authorities to buy books and made the albatross fractionally less offensive by having a penny instead of a halfpenny label attached to it.

In the rest of the country outside Greater London over 80 towns had adopted the Acts by 1880. In contrast, by that date the Metropolis had ignored them entirely except for the combined parishes of St. Margaret and St. John, Westminster. In 1879 the Metropolitan Free Libraries Association was formed with John Jackson, the Bishop of London, as its President, in order to change this situation. Although the 1880's saw the setting up of libraries in many parishes, the whole process was like watching an unwilling carthorse break into a shambling canter rather than a sustained gallop.

The surviving material in the form of posters, handbills and voting returns for adopting the Acts, makes it clear that the householders of London needed a great deal of convincing. However, even in this atmosphere of general unwillingness, it is worth noting that the City of London, whose long perspective of history and life generally has always made the acceptance of innovation agonisingly difficult, was well behind the rest of the field. It opened up the doors of the Guildhall Reference Library to the public for the first time in 1872, when the then new building came into operation, but felt unable to set up lending libraries until 1966, more than a century after this not exactly revolutionary suggestion was first mooted. In mitigation, it ought perhaps to be pointed out that St. Marylebone provided no public library, either reference or lending, until 1923, Paddington adopted the Acts in 1920, but offered no real service until 1930, while Barnes had to wait until 1943 before it could claim to be in business.

Public Libraries and Museums.

NOTICE is hereby given, That in pursuance of the twenty-fourth section of the Act of Parliament of the 18th and 19th Vict., cap. 70, "for further promoting the "establishment of Free Public Libraries and Museums in municipal towns, and for "extending it to towns governed under Local Improvement Acts, and to Parishes," and agreeably to a Resolution of the Court of Common Council, requesting me to convene a Public Meeting of all persons rated and assessed to the Consolidated Rate in the City of London, in order to determine whether the "Public Libraries Act 1855" shall be adopted in the said City, a MEETING will be held in the GUILDHALL of the said City on THURSDAY the 11th day of JULY next, at TWO o'clock precisely, for the above purpose.

WILLIAM CUBITT, Mayor.

Mansion House, 29th June, 1861.

N.B. Ratepayers attending this Meeting are respectfully requested to bring this Notice with them.

Saint Margaret and Saint John the Evangelist, Westminster.

"PUBLIC LIBRARIES ACT 1855."

PURSUANT to a Requisition in writing duly signed as required by the Act, and received by us the undersigned, being the Overseers of the Poor of the said Parishes of Saint Margaret and Saint John the Evangelist, Westminster, on the 1st day of May instant, we do hereby appoint MONDAY the 19th day of May instant, at FOUR o'clock in the Afternoon precisely, at the Mechanics' Institution situate in Great Smith Street, in the said Parish of Saint John the Evangelist, for a Public Meeting of the Ratepayers of the said Parishes of Saint Margaret and Saint John the Evangelist, then and there to determine whether "The Public Libraries Act 1855," shall be adopted for the said Parishes.

Dated this 7th day of May, 1856.

THOMAS GABRIEL BOTTOMLEY,
THOMAS SCUDAMORE,
JOB COOK,
HENRY BEECHER,
Overseers of the Poor of the Parishes of Saint Margaret and Saint John the Evangelist, Westminster.

HAYES, PRINTER, DARTMOUTH STREET.

FREE LIBRARY FOR THE CITY.

Ward of Farringdon Within.

A

PUBLIC MEETING

Will be held in

Christ's Hospital,

NEWGATE STREET,
ON

TUESDAY, MAY 7th,

AT HALF-PAST SEVEN O'CLOCK PRECISELY,

MR. ALDERMAN PHILLIPS

IN THE CHAIR,

For the purpose of promoting the establishment of a Free Library in the City.

Several Gentlemen connected with the Ward will address the Meeting.

The attendance of all interested in the progress of Education is earnestly requested.

W. R. COLLINGRIDGE, City Press, 117 to 119, Aldersgate Street, London, E.C.

Above: Public meetings were convened by those in favour of adopting the Acts. While in some instances the wording was kept low-key and neutral, it is obvious that all available talent was mustered to ensure adoption

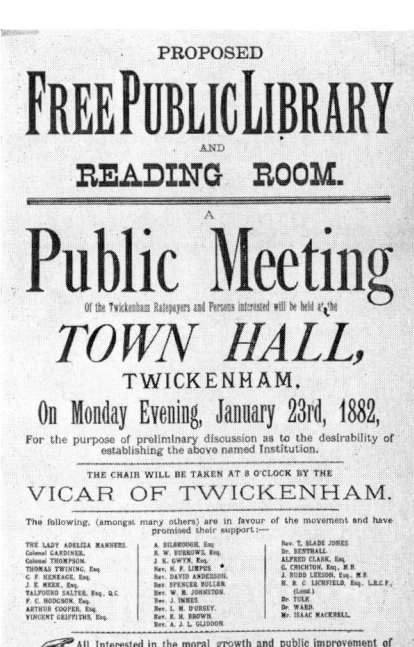
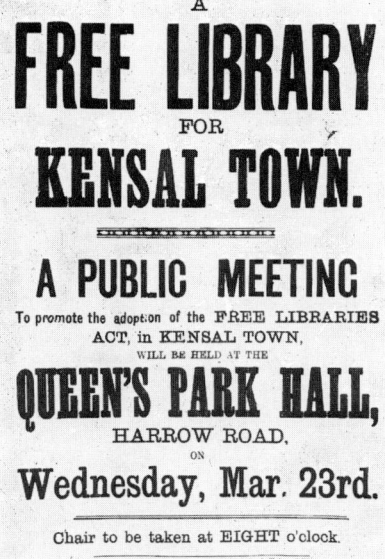

Above: Further notices of meetings to adopt the Acts continued from the previous page and a somewhat muddled handbill at the height of the battle in Clerkenwell

Above: A rather sad little cartoon as ammunition in the fight for the adoption of the Acts. It appears to be of about 1912. However, Barnes only opened a service to the public in 1943, after opting out of Surrey County in 1935

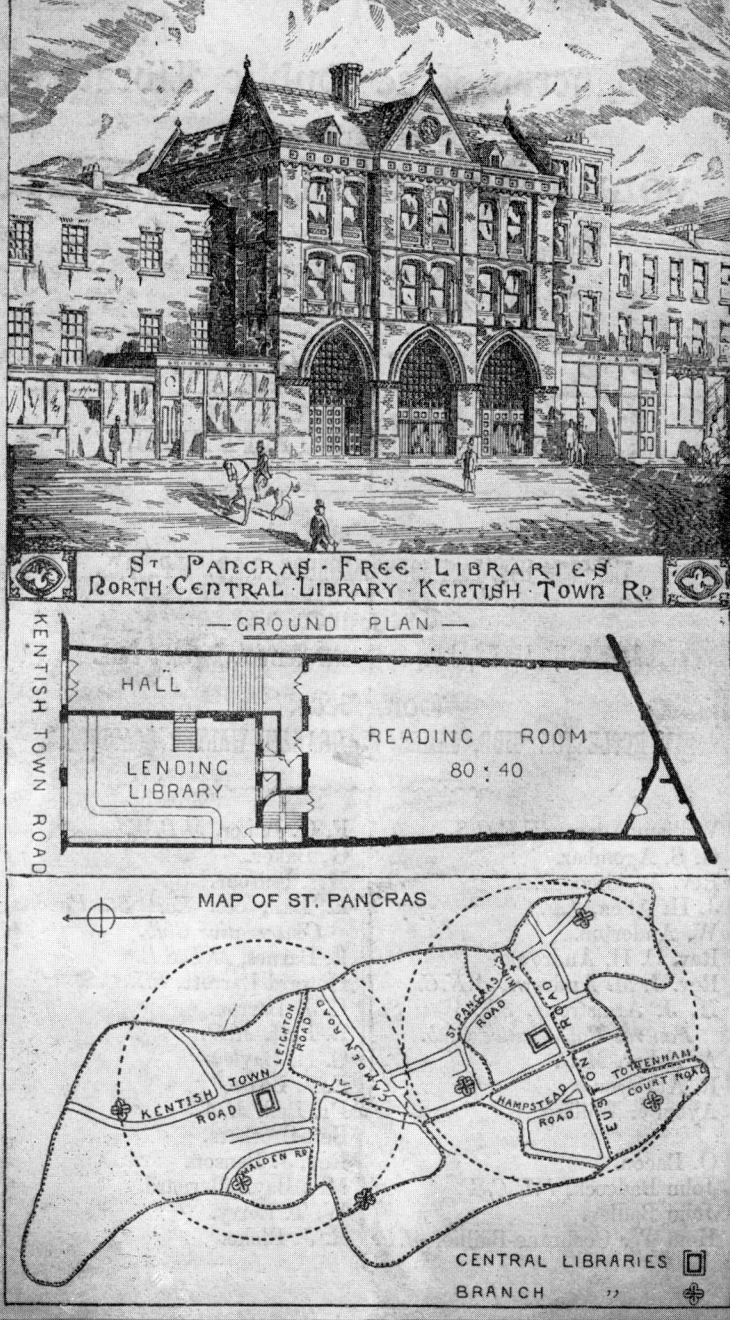

Above: Those trying to promote the public library movement in St. Pancras were often overcome with delusions of grandeur. An ambitious plan for a large Central Library came to nothing in 1906 after a much-publicised competition for designs. This earlier undated proposal, of before 1890, suggested *two* main libraries with three satellite branches for each. The one for the Euston Road was obviously influenced by the proximity of the St. Pancras Hotel while that for Kentish Town has the air of a former prison being used as a fire station. It is pleasant to note that dreams do sometimes come true and that the splendid building housing the Library and Shaw Theatre, opened by the London Borough of Camden in April 1971, is only two hundred yards away from the proposed site in this illustration

ISLINGTON Public Libraries Rejection Association.

Public Libraries for Islington.

10, Prospero Rd., Upper Holloway, N.

Sir (or Madam),

An influential Association of Ratepayers has been formed to OPPOSE the establishment of the above Libraries.

We submit a few reasons why these Libraries should not be established at the expense of the Ratepayers. We trust that you will carefully read them, and give the subject your most careful consideration.

We are now forming and organizing a band of Voluntary Workers to circulate pamphlets, leaflets, &c., and we intend holding Public Meetings throughout the Parish in order to place the facts and figures relating to this subject fully before the Ratepayers.

In order to do this, it will be necessary to obtain the assistance of a large number of workers, and it will of course entail considerable expenses, for which we entirely depend upon voluntary subscriptions. We therefore ask you to help in this work by either joining the Association or subscribing to the funds (no matter how small the amount).

We have not the slightest doubt that when the Ratepayers know how this scheme originated, and how they are being misled by its rate-exploiting advocates, their vote AGAINST will be as decided, or more so, as it was on the three previous occasions.

Look out for your Voting Paper, and DO NOT FAIL TO VOTE "NO!" Voting Papers will be delivered to and collected from your house on January 15th next.

Subscriptions are solicited. May be sent to Mr. W. F. COOTE, 8, Albion Grove, Barnsbury, N.; to any Member of the Committee; or to the Hon. Secretary. A printed receipt will be given.

I am, yours respectfully,
W. J. JONES, Hon. Sec.

ISLINGTON PUBLIC LIBRARIES Rejection Association.

READ THIS, AND PONDER WELL!

On January 15th next, you will be asked to vote "Yes" or "No," as to whether you wish to adopt the Public Libraries Act for this Parish. The Ratepayers have on three previous occasions said "NO!" The last time in 1891.

On the present occasion there has been no wish, desire, or demand made manifest by the Ratepayers to adopt the Act! But a few Vestrymen and their personal friends have started an agitation—for reasons best known to themselves!—and have obtained a promise from Mr. Passmore Edwards to give £10,000 to BUILD (not to furnish and equip) Three Libraries. This they are dangling as a Bait or a Bribe before the Ratepayers to adopt the Act.

Those who are so frantically advocating the establishment of these Libraries are suggesting—nay, even claiming—that they are doing so in the interest of the Working Man, and that the Rate will not exceed One Halfpenny in the Pound!

As there are to be only Three Libraries—i.e., One Library for two square miles—how many working men would be able to walk one or one and half miles to see the evening paper, or borrow a book, after their day's work? At Elections we are told that he has not time to vote, and so the poll is kept open till a late hour for him. If he has not time to go to the poll, will he be able to go to the Public Library?

Again, when we come to the Educational Plea so plausibly adduced on behalf of the young, What do we find? Why, the Evening Continuation and Technical Education Classes at Board Schools are so poorly attended that many have had to be discontinued, notwithstanding that every effort is made to induce the young scholars to attend. These Classes cost the Ratepayers

THOUSANDS OF POUNDS PER ANNUM.

Will the Public Libraries be likely to succeed where these Institutions fail? No! It is the leisured and novel reading classes—as a local newspaper describes them: "The cream of the parish"—who want the Public Libraries, so that they may get their literary recreation at the public expense!

It is not the poor Ratepayer nor the highly rated Tradesmen who want Public Libraries, which are fads, not necessities. It is the duty of Vestrymen to administer the laws; to provide necessities, not luxuries and fads; and to study economy in expending public money.

DON'T FORGET TO VOTE "NO!"

ISLINGTON PUBLIC LIBRARIES REJECTION ASSOCIATION.

Twelve Reasons Against Public Libraries.

Because they are Not necessities.

Because the Ratepayers have not shewn any desire to have them.

Because they have already been voted against three times

Because the reasons given by the advocates are not true.

Because literature is cheap enough for every one to buy his own books if he wants them.

Because the Rates already provide education, and plenty of it, for the young.

Because it is only a Fad of a clique of Vestrymen.

Because 24,709 summonses were issued last year against ratepayers who could not pay their rates.

Because it is misleading to say that Libraries are for the benefit of the poor; they are more for the pleasure of the rich.

Because Mr. Passmore Edwards' offer will only provide the empty buildings, but not the freehold.

Because a rate of One Penny in the Pound would only provide and furnish library accommodation for a small portion of the 336,764 inhabitants, and it is only a misstatement for the advocates to pretend that a halfpenny will do.

Because, in short, the whole scheme is a farce, a delusion and a snare to further impoverish the already over-burdened ratepayers; and is nothing more nor less than a BRIBE to the ratepayers.

Above: Strong opposition from Islington

MORE TAXES WANTED FOR THE LIBRARIES.

One Penny in the Pound.

There are upwards of 750,000 lazy, idle people in Lambeth, reading themselves blind, silly, round shouldered, and bringing on chest disease and consumption, at the hardworking ratepayers expense, and we are to increase that number. If the rich want them let them pay for or endow them, and not call upon the poor hardworking ratepayers.

Note—No person can get books without the security from a substantial ratepayer. This 1d. rate will have to be paid by the poor tenant in the end. It is no good to them.

Put "NO" to the Voting Paper.

Please put this in the Window.

VOTERS OF CHELSEA.

If you do not wish the oppressive burden of your Rates increased, say **NO** to the Free Library Scheme.

If you do not wish to injure those Tradesmen who sell and lend Newspapers and Novels say **NO** to the Free Library Scheme.

If you think the Metropolis already sufficiently supplied with National Free Libraries say **NO** to the Free Library Scheme.

If you think Paddington, Islington, West Ham, Woolwich, Plumstead, and other great Districts of the Metropolis right when they rejected the Free Libraries this year, say **NO** to the Chelsea Free Library Scheme.

If you think your own Representatives upon the Chelsea Vestry right when they disapproved of a Free Library in our midst, say **NO** emphatically to the Free Library Scheme.

Look out for the VOTING PAPERS delivered to-day and mark them **NO**.

A RATEPAYER.

13th May, 1887.

Above: It is clear from these two handbills that Chelsea and Lambeth were not far behind Islington

"CASTING PEARLS—"

Marylebone Bumble (to Mr. C-rn-gie). "GO AWAY, MY GOOD FELLER! WE DON'T WANT NO BOOKS 'ERE!"

["Marylebone is not going to allow itself to be bribed, even by Mr. CARNEGIE, to encourage reading within its borders, and so it has declined that gentleman's offer of £30,000 for the provision of free libraries."—*Westminster Gazette*, Oct. 1.]

Above: St. Marylebone was an even more hardened objector than Islington, Chelsea and Lambeth and opened no service until 1923. Here a *Punch* cartoon of October 2nd, 1902 puts the matter in perspective when Andrew Carnegie's offer of help was rejected

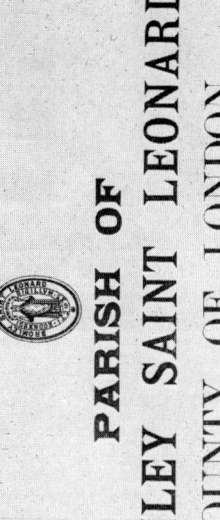

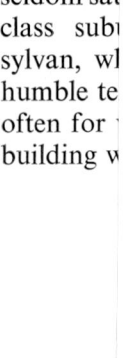

Above: The actual vote and result in Bromley St. Leonard

Above: The first library provided by East Ham. This was in Station Street in North Woolwich and opened in 1896, although the photograph is undated. The curious chimneys suggest that a boiler for a small heating system had been installed. The library was presumably in use until 1929 when a branch was opened in the nearby Rymill Street. In turn, this has now been replaced by a modern building in Pier Road

Above: The Limes was situated in High Street North, East Ham and had an extremely short life even for temporary premises. It was opened on January 2nd, 1899 and superseded by the Plashet Grove Branch opened on October 28th of the same year

Above: These buildings occupied the site of the present Hammersmith Central Library, which was opened on July 24th, 1905. The house on the left with an entrance like a sentry box served as a temporary reading room from January 1st, 1902 until the clearing of the site for building early in 1904

30

Above: Rosebank was a private house used as the first Walthamstow Central Library. It was opened on September 29th, 1894 with a new reading room added at the back. Rosebank was demolished to make way for the then new Central Library on the same site, which was opened on July 10th, 1909, and still serves the London Borough of Waltham Forest in the same capacity. The 1894 reading room was incorporated into the fabric of the 1909 building. This photograph is of 1908

Above: Rokeby House, an early Jacobean building, served as the first West Ham Central Library from its opening, originally as a newsroom only, on 30th July, 1892 until its demolition in 1898. It was situated in Stratford Broadway and its valuable oak panelling was acquired by the Victoria and Albert Museum. The photograph is undated, but appears to be of October or November 1892. The custom-built replacement in Water Lane opened on October 6th, 1898

Right: This shop served as the Highams Park Branch of Walthamstow Public Libraries from 1896 to February 1902. It has all the gay abandon of an undertaker's, an impression reinforced by the mock-marble columns on either side of the shop windows

31

Benefactors

Reference has already been made to the slowness of the adoption of the Acts in Greater London and if a number of benefactors had not come forward and offered sites, buildings and to a lesser extent, donations of books, it seems extremely doubtful whether the public library movement would ever have really succeeded in making headway in some areas of the Metropolis.

By far the most outstanding donor in London, as in most other parts of the world, was Andrew Carnegie (1835–1919), the American steel millionaire. The only other person who came near this abundance, was John Passmore Edwards (1823–1911), who was responsible for eight libraries in his native Cornwall in the 1890's and fifteen in Greater London from 1890 to 1903.

Interesting donors of individual buildings were Sir George Newnes, the newspaper proprietor, at Putney, Sir Henry Tate, the sugar magnate, at Lambeth and Sir George Livesey, Engineer and Secretary of the South Metropolitan Gas Company, at Camberwell, opposite the Company's premises near the junction of Old Kent Road and Commercial Way. The latter produced an unfortunate example of biting the hand that feeds you, as the Camberwell Library Commissioners would only allow employees of the South Metropolitan Gas Company to use the building, if they were also Camberwell residents. This happened apparently after the Clerk to the Commissioners had given his legal opinion on the matter. Within a month, however, the Commissioners changed their minds. This was perhaps not surprising as Sir George himself was a Commissioner and doubtless an experienced and formidable lobbyist. The library in question is now a museum.

A donation somewhat out of the ordinary was that of William Minet, in the then border area between Lambeth and Camberwell. He gave land and a library building to be used equally by all people on his estates, which extended over the boundary between both districts. This was an enlightened move at a time when it was not legally possible for parishes to combine in the provision of library services. It continued as a joint venture until 1956, when Lambeth assumed total responsibility for the building, which had been reconstructed after war damage.

Above: Authorised photographs of the two big spenders. These were used extensively in brochures for stone-laying and opening ceremonies. On the left Andrew Carnegie, and on the right John Passmore Edwards

Right: Terra-cotta plaque over the main entrance of the Borough Road Library, Southwark. It is a strange mixture of Art Nouveau and Jacobean strapwork decoration.
Architects: C. J. Phipps and A. Blomfield Jackson

Above: There are more ways to honour a benefactor than by putting up a plaque. The musical selection at the laying of the foundation stone at Hanwell on November 26th, 1904 included a large proportion of American tunes in honour of Andrew Carnegie. *Architect:* T. Gibbs Thomas

Right: The plaque at Putney Library commemorating the gift of the site and building by Sir George Newnes. *Architect:* F. J. Smith

Above: James Heywood was a little-known benefactor, who set up a library at his own expense in Kensington. This was situated in a shop at 106 High Street, Notting Hill Gate, and flourished from 1874 to 1891. It was taken over as a municipal institution on January 2nd, 1888 and one of the members of its staff, Herbert Jones, became Kensington's first Librarian. It did not finally close until the opening of the North Kensington Branch on October 29th, 1891

Above: John Passmore Edwards at the opening of the Hammersmith Branch Library at Shepherds Bush on June 25th, 1896. He is the venerable bearded figure in the entrance directly below the keystone of the arch and the plaque bearing his name. For a view of a less formal aspect of this building, see page 99. *Architect:* Maurice Adams

Right: Although a generous donor, John Passmore Edwards can hardly be placed high in the pantheon of English poets, as this sonnet reveals. It was composed for the opening of Rosebank on September 29th, 1894 (see the photograph on page 31). In extenuation, it should be pointed out that Passmore Edwards was over 70 at the time he wrote it. The 'stately pile' refers to the new reading room constructed behind Rosebank, which was incorporated into the 1909 Central Library

---

A SONNET

on the

OPENING OF THE

WALTHAMSTOW PUBLIC LIBRARY,

by

J. Passmore Edwards Esq.

Ye citizens of Walthamstow rejoice!
Within your midst a stately pile arises,
And, with its beauty, all your hearts surprises:
Then greet its opening with a gladsome voice!
As light reveals the beauty of the earth,
And penetrates the realms of endless space:—
So may the books within this glorious place
Disclose to men the deeds of greatest worth!
Here all who care may read our nation's story
And drink from "wells of English undefiled".
Within these walls Truth shall have greatest glory
Error shall be dethroned and Vice exiled!
Though fierce and loud the storm may rage around.
Here at all times may smiling Peace be found!

Above: Knowing which side your bread is buttered. A dinner held by the Library Association in honour of Andrew Carnegie at the Hotel Cecil in the Strand on June 2nd, 1913. Carnegie is the small bearded figure standing directly beneath the centre of the third big mirror from the right. The somewhat larger

figure standing immediately beneath the right hand edge of the same mirror is Frank J. Leslie, the then President of the Library Association and Chairman of the Liverpool Public Libraries Committee

Above: Is this a record? What must have been one of the largest gatherings of its kind met at the junction of Romford Road and Water Lane, West Ham, on October 29th, 1896 to witness Alderman W. Crow, J.P., Mayor of the Borough, lay the foundation stone of the new Central Library and Technical

Institute. The stone is particularly elaborate and what at first sight appears to be a police band providing appropriate music in a somewhat misty background is in fact that of the 4th Essex Volunteers. See page 52 for the subsequent opening ceremony. *Architects:* Gibson and Russell

Right: The stone-laying ceremony at Manor Park Library, East Ham, on June 2nd, 1904, when John Passmore Edwards was over eighty. His unmistakable figure in flowing white locks and beard stands proudly near the stone with hat in hand and umbrella over the arm. The clarity of the photograph is remarkable with the thumbnail of Passmore Edwards' unencumbered hand clearly visible. The Library is situated in Romford Road at the junction with Rabbits Road (see page 65 for an exterior view) and the opening ceremony was performed on August 3rd, 1905. *Architect:* A. Horsburgh Campbell

40

Above: Laying the foundation stone at Chelsea Library on February 8th, 1890. Note the small boy in sailor suit placing a hand on the stone itself, while his elders and betters are preoccupied with the photographer. The opening ceremony was performed on January 21st, 1891. *Architect:* John Brydon
Below: Hampstead Central Library at the junction of Finchley Road and Arkwright Road with Henry Harben, who met the cost of the building, laying the foundation stone on November 10th, 1896. The opening ceremony took place on November 10th, 1897, and the building, which was damaged by bombing in the second world war, now serves as the Camden Arts Centre. *Architect:* Arnold S. Tayler

Right: The stone-laying ceremony of the Belsize Branch in Antrim Road, Hampstead, which took place on August 10th, 1896. The opening ceremony followed on April 10th, 1897. The structure was declared unsafe in 1936 and replaced by the present building of 1937. *Architect of Original Building:* Charles H. Lowe, Surveyor to the Vestry

"LIBRARIES ARE AS THE SHRINES WHERE ALL THE RELICS OF THE ANCIENT SAINTS, FULL OF TRUE VIRTUE, AND THAT WITHOUT DELUSION OR IMPOSTURE, ARE PRESERVED AND REPOSED."—BACON

THE CHAIRMAN OF THE COUNCIL (Councillor H. HEATHER, J.P.), will take the Chair.

THE REV. J. T. INSKIP, M.A., Vicar of Leyton, will offer Prayer.

THE ARCHITECT (Mr. William Jacques, A.R.I.B.A.), will briefly explain the designs, and present a Silver Trowel to Mr. Golightly.

THE CHAIRMAN will ask Councillor Golightly to Lay the Memorial Stone.

Councillor Golightly will Lay the Stone.

A VOTE OF THANKS to Mr. Golightly will be proposed by Councillor Musgrave, E.C.C., and seconded by Councillor Tomlins.

COUNCILLOR GOLIGHTLY will acknowledge the same.

COUNCILLOR PITTAM will propose "That the best thanks of the inhabitants of the Urban District of Leyton be accorded to MR. ANDREW CARNEGIE, LL.D., for presenting the District with two handsome Libraries."

COUNCILLOR T. W. MITCHELL will second the same.

E. J. DAVIS, ESQ., E.C.C., will support the Resolution.

COUNCILLOR TRUMBLE will propose "That the best thanks of the inhabitants of Leyton be accorded to Mr. Edward Jones, for presenting the Site for the Lea Bridge Branch Library."

COUNCILLOR BUSSEY will second the same.

BENJAMIN BIGGS, ESQ., will support the Resolution.

COUNCILLOR SLADE will propose a Vote of Thanks to the Chairman.

COUNCILLOR HURRY will second the same.

THE CHAIRMAN will reply.

Above: A typical Edwardian stone-laying programme. This one was produced for the ceremony at Lea Bridge Library, Leyton, on September 30th, 1905. The thistle motif in the decoration at the top of the page was used in deference to Andrew Carnegie's Scottish ancestry
Below: Twickenham Library. The laying of the foundation stone on June 18th, 1906. The Library was subsequently opened on March 20th, 1907. The man in the boater standing on the scaffolding has a rather Max Millerish air about him. Surely he must be from the building firm rather than one of the important personages assembled below? *Architect:* Howard Goadby

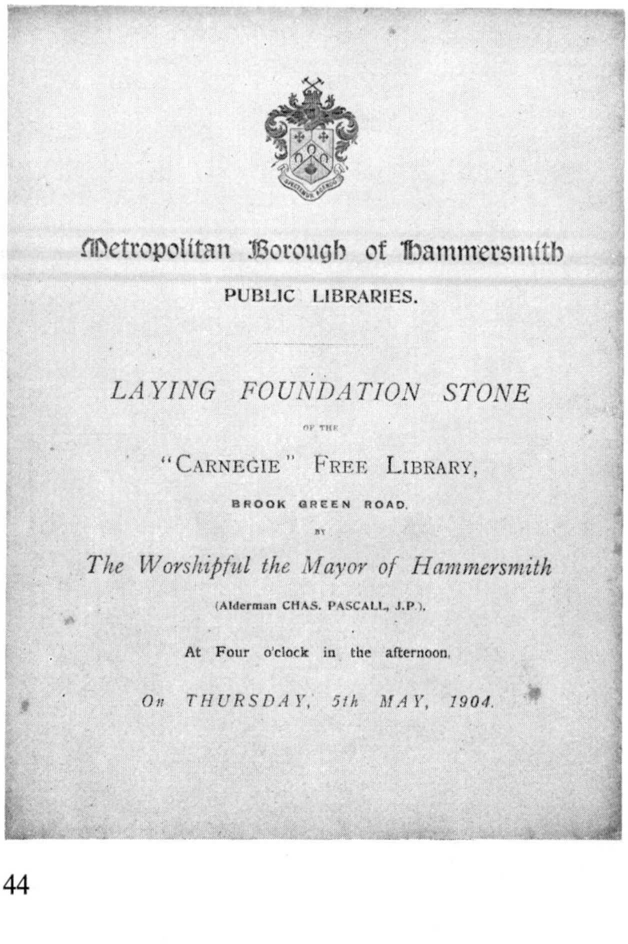

Above: The stone-laying ceremony for Hammersmith Central Library on May 5th, 1904. The Mayor and Town Clerk were unable to stand still for the photographer, although the mace bearer, used no doubt to Services' discipline, finds no difficulty at all. The gentlemen on the left in bowler hats appear to be journalists. The ladies are relegated to a fuzzy obscurity on the extreme left, while the blur at the front is presumably the feather of a particularly large and imposing hat

Metropolitan Borough of Hammersmith

PUBLIC LIBRARIES.

LAYING FOUNDATION STONE

OF THE

"CARNEGIE" FREE LIBRARY,

BROOK GREEN ROAD,

BY

The Worshipful the Mayor of Hammersmith

(Alderman CHAS. PASCALL, J.P.).

At Four o'clock in the afternoon.

On THURSDAY, 5th MAY, 1904.

Left: The programme for the ceremony

44

Opening Ceremonies

The opening of a library was clearly a much grander affair than the stone laying. As the building was now finished, the ceremony could at least take place inside without any worries about the vagaries of the weather.

From an early hour, men from the Parks Department laboured mightily with potted palms, banks of flowers and suitable bunting, to conceal a raised dais for the speeches. These were as long, exhortatory and full of literary allusion, as those at the stone laying ceremony, and reported at even greater length in the local press. The building tended to be characterised as 'a temple of learning' and was thought to offer more alluring attractions 'than those supplied by the Brewers'. Phrases of the latter kind tended to be greated by 'hear, hear' or 'loud applause'. The Brewers themselves never went on record as feeling that this hit below the belt, presumably because they had done their market research thoroughly, and knew that those who frequented public libraries and public houses were not mutually exclusive groups.

It was an occasion for both men and women to put on their finery, and a place on the platform was sought after with some eagerness. The Distinguished Person performing the actual ceremony was usually in the centre, flanked by the Mayor and Town Clerk. The wives of this trio took their station to either side, with the rest of the Libraries Committee and *their* wives behind or even further to the side. If seating arrangements had not been made with due attention, some unfortunates were herded behind the potted palms, through which they peered either in rage or bewilderment, rather like the animals in a painting by *Le Douanier Rousseau*.

At the end of the ceremony, similar refreshments to the stone laying would be provided, or, if the guests were fortunate, a full-blown mayoral reception was laid on the same evening. The day's proceedings were usually recorded for posterity on a commemorative plaque, bearing the names of the Distinguished Opener, the Mayor, the members of the Libraries Committee, the Town Clerk, the Architect and the Builder. If the name of the Librarian was added to this impressive list, it was usually only at the very end.

Above: On returning to earth, Russian cosmonauts participate in an elaborate ceremony including a walk down a long red carpet. At the opening of Hackney Central Library on May 28th, 1908, the photographer managed to catch the moments before the Prince and Princess of Wales (later to become George V and Queen Mary) did the same thing as part of the day's proceedings. *Architect:* H. A. Crouch

Above: The opening of the Lambeth Central Library at Brixton Oval on March 4th, 1893 by the Prince of Wales. The building was the gift of Henry (later Sir Henry) Tate, who is seen in the illustration handing the title deeds to the Prince. The illustration is from the *Daily Graphic* of March 6th, 1893. *Architect:* Sidney R. J. Smith

Below: The Prince That Never Was. The carriage which brought the Prince and Princess of Wales to the Lambeth Central Library for the opening ceremony. As a photograph, it is a total disaster. Neither the Prince nor Princess of Wales appear, the driver can only just be discerned and one horse very inconsiderately moved. The guard of honour was provided by the 4th V.B. Queen's West Surreys, 'together with a contingent of its smart cyclists and the regimental band'. An arch formed by two fire escapes, with attendant firemen, also stood in Rushfield Road (at that time Ardville Road) near the main entrance of the building. See the next page for poems about the whole event

Welcome, Albert Edward,
Our noble Prince of Wales,
To open Tate's great gift to us,
Which all of us will hail
With gladsome glee and wishes,
To such great men of zest,
We wish him every happiness,
And his long name be blessed.

On March the Fourth now close at hand
The Prince of Wales will open free,
Tate's noble gift so bold and grand
The Brixton Central Library.

To honour them we must awake,
For Brixtonites are very slow,
And see for once if we can't make
A really brilliant public show.

Raise up a grand Triumphal Arch
With flags and banners decorate,
To welcome on the Fourth of March,
The Prince of Wales and Henry Tate.

Above: The great day recorded on the previous page obviously inspired the local writers of doggerel to unplumbed depths of banality and two anonymous poems that appeared in the *Brixton Free Press* are reproduced as delightful period pieces. To describe the Prince as 'a great man of zest', might be thought an artful and subtle dig at his amorous adventures, if it were not patently clear that the writer had not a whit of artifice or subtlety in him. As for 'The Prince of Wales will open free', it could be construed that he normally charged a fee, which was being waived on this occasion

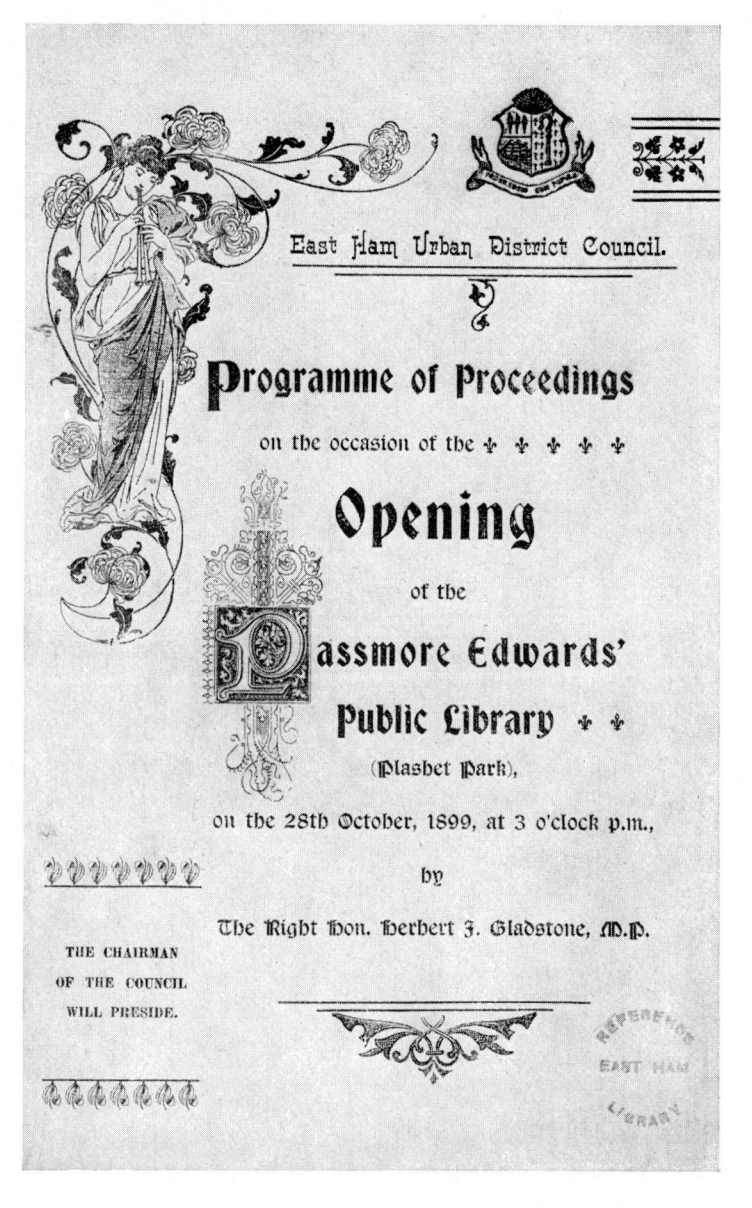

Right: A splendid piece of Arts and Crafts design for the opening of the East Ham Branch at Plashet Park on October 28th, 1899. *Architect:* Silvanus Trevail, who was also responsible for a large number of Passmore Edwards' buildings in Cornwall

Right: Brentford Central Library was opened on May 9th, 1904 by Andrew Carnegie, who sits in the middle of the front row. Second from the left in the front row is the local M.P., James Bigwood, resplendent in grey spats. A north-easterly line from Carnegie passes through Fred Turner, the Librarian and secondly Nowell Parr, the architect of the building. Turner was one of those people with the facility for charming birds off the trees and Carnegie was so impressed with all the arrangements for the opening, that he offered on the spot to pay for the furniture and fittings in addition to the fabric of the building. Turner reached the ripe old age of 94 and did not die until 1959. The tall gentleman holding a top hat, second from the right in the second row, is Professor MacNeile Dixon, the then President of the Library Association. Third from the left, also in the second row is J. Bertram, Carnegie's hard-working and self-effacing secretary, who is sandwiched between two local doctors, one plump and prosperous, the other faintly abstracted. The uniformed personage at the extreme left, who looks like a cross between a Belgian station-master and a Salvation Army bandsman, is the Head Caretaker. *Architect*: Nowell Parr

48

PROGRAMME

Part Song ... "Watch her kindly" ... *Buck*	Speech— Mr. W. PELHAM BULLIVANT, J.P., *Chairman of the Commissioners.*
THE VERNON LEE PART SINGERS.	Speech— Mr. SYDNEY BUXTON, M.P.
Song ... "The Holy City" ... *Adams*	Quartette ... "Annie Laurie" ... *S.A.*
Mr. HERBERT EMLYN.	THE VERNON LEE PART SINGERS.
Song ... "She wandered down the mountain side" ... *Clay*	Song ... "Trifle not with love" (La Cigale) ... *Cellier*
Miss MARY HARRIS.	Mr. HERBERT EMLYN.
Song ... "Ailsa, Mine" ... *Newton*	Song ... "Scenes that are brightest" (Maritana) ... *Wallace*
Mr. JAMES BECKWITH.	Miss MARY HARRIS.
Song ... "The Pilgrim of Love" ... *Bishop*	Part Song ... "The Ash Grove" ... *Cozens*
Mr. WILLIAM FELL.	THE VERNON LEE PART SINGERS.
Song ... "Ninety years ago" ... *A.L.*	Song ... "On the blue Atlantic" ... *Newton*
Miss MINNIE CHAMBERLAIN.	Mr. WINGROVE IVES.
Song ... "The Whirlwind" ... *Attewater*	Song ... "So fare thee well" (Doris) ... *Cellier*
Mr. WINGROVE IVES.	Mr. WILLIAM FELL.
Humorous Part Song "Simple Simon" ... *S.A.*	Song ... "The hum of Bees" ... *Marzials*
THE VERNON LEE PART SINGERS.	Miss MINNIE CHAMBERLAIN.
	Humorous Song ... (Selected) ...
	Mr. FRED H. COZENS.
	Part Song ... "The long day closes" ... *Sullivan*
	THE VERNON LEE PART SINGERS.

NATIONAL ANTHEM.

Above: The Poplar Commissioners had problems when they were choosing somebody to open the building at 126 Poplar High Street. A. J. Balfour, Lord Rosebery and Lord Kelvin all refused one after another and so it was decided to substitute a musical entertainment, which was thoroughly enjoyed by all who attended. The Commissioners no doubt heaved a collective sigh of relief as the most appropriate final item was performed by the Vernon Lee Part Singers. The building was bombed in the second world war, but survived as a library until 1957, when it was bought by the L.C.C. as an extension to Poplar Technical College. The service in the area was taken over by the Lansbury Library, which was built as a replacement in Market Way. *Architects of High Street Library:* J. & S. F. Clarkson

Below: The memorial tablet for the opening of Poplar High Street Library, a ceremony which eventually had to be performed by the Chairman of the Commissioners

Below: The memorial tablet for the opening of North Kensington Library with rather more aristocratic commissioners. For more details of this most interesting building see page 67

Right: Kingston upon Thames Central Library was opened on May 11th, 1903 by Andrew Carnegie, who stands with rolled umbrella next to the Mayor and Mayoress as an anxious member of staff peers out of the window at the distinguished guests. J. Bertram, Carnegie's private secretary appears in this photograph, as in the one of the opening of Brentford Central Library on page 48. He is the small, dark figure directly above the floral decoration in the hat of the Mayoress. *Architect*: Alfred Cox

THE MAYOR & MAYORESS
OF ISLINGTON

(ALDERMAN GEO. S. ELLIOTT, J.P.,
AND MRS. ELLIOTT.)

Reception and Dance

AT THE

CENTRAL LIBRARY, ISLINGTON
Thursday, 24th October, 1907.

9 P.M. TILL 2 A.M.

Refreshments
will be served in the Reference Library

Menu.

Consommé de Volaille.
Sandwiches au Poulet, Foie-Gras, Jambon,
et à la Langue.
Petits Pains à la Française.
Bouchées à la Victoria.
Canapes aux Anchois.
Mousseline de Gibier à la St. Hubert.
Condé aux Amandes.
Gâteau Royal.
Baba aux Liqueurs.
Gelées aux Fruits.
Crême Pralinée.
Charlotte à la Moscovite.
Glaces à la Renaissance.
Petit Fours.

Hot House Grapes, Pines, &c.

Thé. Café. Lemonade. Orangeade.
Champagne Cup. Claret Cup.
Marcobrunner. Whiskey. Brandy.

Above: Islington had been one of the foremost districts in London to resist the Acts (see page 18), but when the Central Library was finally opened on October 24th, 1907, it was done in great style with the band of the Coldstream Guards providing the music for a grand evening reception and dance. The Editor of the *Islington Post* assumed that by some oversight he had not received an invitation, but on arrival he was ejected by the police. In a later editorial he put it all down to political prejudice. *Architect:* Henry T. Hare

Below: W. E. Gladstone opening the St. Martin's Library on February 12th, 1891, from the February 21st, 1891 edition of *Pictorial News*. (See page 37 for the stone-laying ceremony and details of the building.) There seems to be a deal of chattering in the assembled throng and presumably the two seated figures, directly behind the young man presenting Gladstone with the first book borrowed, are reporters and not card players. In the top left of the illustration the G.O.M. appears to be exerting considerable pressure to turn the key in the lock

---

St. Martin-in-the-Fields
Free Public Library.

PROGRAMME OF PROCEEDINGS

AT THE OPENING OF THE

LIBRARY BY THE

Rt. Hon. W. E. Gladstone, M.P.

at 2 p.m.

12th FEBRUARY, 1891.

51

Right: October 6th, 1898 saw the opening by John Passmore Edwards of the Central Library and Technical Institute, West Ham, at the junction of Romford Road and Water Lane. (See pages 38 and 39 for the stone-laying ceremony.) Passmore Edwards stands in the front row under the left hand caryatid, which seems somewhat bored by the whole proceedings. Moving right from Passmore Edwards, there stand in succession, Alfred Cotgreave, Librarian of West Ham and the great advocate of indicators and closed access, A. E. Briscoe, Principal of the Technical Institute, Alderman Ivey, Mayor of West Ham and W. Crow, Mayor at the time of the stone-laying. *Architects:* Gibson and Russell

Woburn Abbey.

15th August 1899.

Dear Sir,

I regret that, owing to my absence in Scotland, I shall be unable to preside on October 21st at the interesting ceremony of opening the Hornsey Central Library.

I trust that the successful effort, which you are making to put good libraries within the reach of the inhabitants of the Hornsey District, will be rewarded by the intelligent appreciation of the public for whom they are intended.

Yours truly,

Bedford

Henry Burt Esq
Rhianva
Hornsey Lane.
N.

Legation of the United States
London June 8th 1881.

Sir,

I am very sorry that my engagements are so many and so onerous that I must deny myself the pleasure of being present at the opening of the Richmond Free Library. I would have been glad, I need hardly say, to support Lady Russell, with whose acquaintance I have been honoured for many years.

I remain,
Your obedient servant,

J. R. Lowell.

Frederick Trevor Esq.
Free Public Library
Richmond, Surrey.

Above: Two important refusals to attend openings of libraries. On the left the Duke of Bedford declines an invitation to open Hornsey Central Library, while on the right, J. R. Lowell, poet, critic and noted humanitarian, who was also U.S. Ambassador to the Court of St. James from 1880 to 1885, regrets that he is unable to be present at the opening of Richmond Central Library on June 18th, 1881. *Architect – Hornsey:* E. J. Lovegrove, Engineer and Surveyor to Hornsey U.D.C. (A new library was built as a replacement in 1965.) *Architect – Richmond:* F. S. Brunton

Below: Two rather more humble communications accepting invitations for the opening of Erith Central Library on April 7th, 1906. *Architect:* W. Egerton

---

TELEPHONE (NAT.) No. 26 ERITH.

URBAN DISTRICT COUNCIL OF ERITH

ARTHUR COVENEY,
TRAMWAY ENGINEER AND
GENERAL MANAGER.

Tramway Depot and Offices,
Walnut Tree Road,
Erith, S.E. March 30th, 1906.

Mr. Coveney has great pleasure in accepting Mr. Councillor Ling's invitation to be present at the opening of the Erith Library on the 7th proximo.

TELEPHONE (NAT.) NO. 7. ERITH.

A. SAUNDERS.

URBAN DISTRICT COUNCIL OF ERITH

INSPECTOR OF NUISANCES.

Bexley Road,
Erith, Kent.
4 April 1906

The Librarian
Free Library
Erith

Dear Sir

I accept with thanks the invitation of Mr Councillor Ling & Committee to the opening of the Free Library on Saturday 7th inst

Yours faithfully
A Saunders
Inspr of Nuisances

Above: The opening of Rosebank on September 29th, 1894 (see also page 31) by John Passmore Edwards, who sits in patriarchial manner behind the table. The lighting fitments look as if they might well have been a caretaker's nightmare

Below: Walthamstow Central Library was opened on July 10th, 1909 by John Simon (1873–1954), M.P. for Walthamstow from 1906 to 1918. In 1910 he was knighted and appointed Solicitor-General. His wife had died in 1902 when he was still under thirty and his natural reserve was deepened by this tragedy. In this photograph he stands looking sad, pensive and withdrawn. In contrast, the clerical gentleman on the extreme left of the platform appears simply annoyed in his fight with the potted palm

Right: Wood Green Central Library was opened on September 28th, 1907 and demolished in 1973 to make way for a newer building. The opening ceremony was performed by Ernest Oliver, Chairman of the Libraries Committee. He ran into a spot of bother, as he had sent out the invitations in the name of the Chairman and Committee, although some members of the Committee said that they had not been involved in making the arrangements and promptly boycotted the proceedings. A tram was hired to take the ladies to the Library from the Town Hall, where they had assembled. The men however were not so lucky and had to walk. The building had been constructed with the aid of a large grant from Andrew Carnegie, and Councillor Cole, who moved the vote of thanks for this munificence, suggested it should be sent as swiftly as possible in the hope that it would induce Carnegie to build a library at Alexandra Park. Councillor Holmes, who seconded the vote, pointed out that it would be unfair to blame Carnegie for being a millionaire and Wood Green also needed some public baths, the upkeep of which would only be half as much as the Library. One of the jobs of juniors was winding the turret clock. Overleaf is a photograph taken after the ceremony at the Town Hall, just before the serving of refreshments. The catering staff are looking out of the window, no doubt in an effort to size up the assembled dignitaries in terms of cress sandwiches and cakes likely to be consumed

Above: A photograph of the original Central Library in Tweedy Road, Bromley (Kent), which was opened on December 8th, 1894 by Sir John Lubbock, M.P., a man much in demand for ceremonies of this kind. The tower and spire are a free adaptation from St. Magnus the Martyr. In the early Edwardian period, the Library was considered too small by the then Bromley U.D.C. A new building was therefore opened in Bromley High Street on May 28th, 1906 by Andrew Carnegie. This was again considered too small and extended in 1912. When the London Borough of Bromley looked into its library provision after 1965, it decided that the High Street Library was once more far too small, but that the site was excellent. The 1906/1912 building was accordingly demolished to allow a new Central Library to be erected. The Tweedy Road building was still available and in March 1968 was taken over again as a temporary expedient. Since that date the new Central Library has been under construction, and has only just been completed. This photograph is of about 1900. As the Lombardic style Baptist Church of 1864 by R. H. Moore is still extant, the usage of the buildings remained exactly the same until April 1977. *Architects of the Tweedy Road Library:* Potts Son and Hennings. *Architect of the 1906/1912 High Street Library:* Evelyn Hellicar

Above: Hampstead Central Library was opened on November 10th, 1897. It stands at the junction of Finchley and Arkwright Roads and now serves as the Camden Arts Centre. By a very enlightened and enterprising piece of management, the Hampstead Vestry bought the whole 8000 volumes of the private library of Henry Morley, Professor of English at University College, London, and this formed the basis of the Reference Library. The building has both an ecclesiastical and academic air about it and looks rather like the training college of a Nonconformist denomination. Indeed, the elevation to Arkwright Road has the appearance of a college chapel, but the roof lights would need modification. *Architect:* Arnold S. Tayler

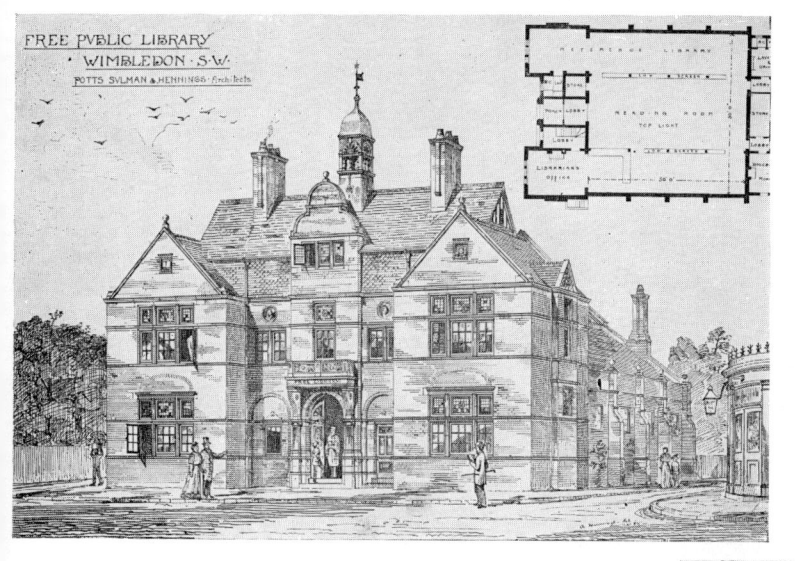

Left: There seems little to say about Wimbledon Library, except that it is remarkably like a very plain private house tarted up with a turret, fancy entrance and Dutch gable. The pub on the corner in this undated print appears altogether more lively. It stands in Wimbledon Hill Road and is still one of the principal libraries of the London Borough of Merton. The opening was performed by Sir John Lubbock, M.P., on March 9th, 1887. *Architects:* Potts, Sulman and Hennings

Right: Richmond was the second area in Greater London outside Westminster to adopt the Acts and the Central Library was opened on June 18th, 1881. In this undated sketch, it has the forthright and uninspired air of a utilitarian vicarage by one of the followers of G. E. Street. It still serves as the Central Library for the London Borough of Richmond upon Thames. *Architect:* F. S. Brunton

Left: Kingston upon Thames Central Library in Fairfield Road. It was opened on May 11th, 1903 and is an Edwardian version of what one of the followers of Wren might have produced in the latter half of the seventeenth century. The building is rather like a prim dowager duchess with a racy past, as the front elevation is highly dignified with the jolly bits reserved for the side and the back. The photograph was taken close to the opening date. *Architect:* Alfred Cox

Above: The site of Whitechapel Library being cleared for construction work on the building. A photograph of 1890

Right: The building itself was opened on October 25th, 1892 by Lord Rosebery and looks a little like a house for a prosperous City merchant. It has general Jacobean and Artisan Mannerist detailing finished off with a free imitation of the turret of St. Botolph's, Aldersgate. An undated phototint, which appears in *Passmore Edwards Institutions* by J. J. Macdonald (Strand Newspaper Co., 1900). *Architects:* Potts, Son and Hennings

Below: As Dulwich Library was conceived by John Passmore Edwards as a memorial to Edward Alleyn, the Elizabethan actor and founder of both Alleyn's School and Dulwich College, it was only natural that the foundation stone should be laid by Sir Henry Irving on September 24th, 1896. In the following year on November 24th, Lord Chancellor Halsbury declared the building open. The ground floor on the left seems to owe something to Richard Norman Shaw's First Alliance Assurance Building in Pall Mall and possibly to the work of the London School Board. The first floor and central section appear to be a pastiche of Elizabethan and Artisan Mannerist elements, while the right hand block is a little like a Quaker meeting house. This sketch is by R. S. Ayling and appeared in *Building News* on October 23rd, 1896. *Architects:* Charles Barry & Son

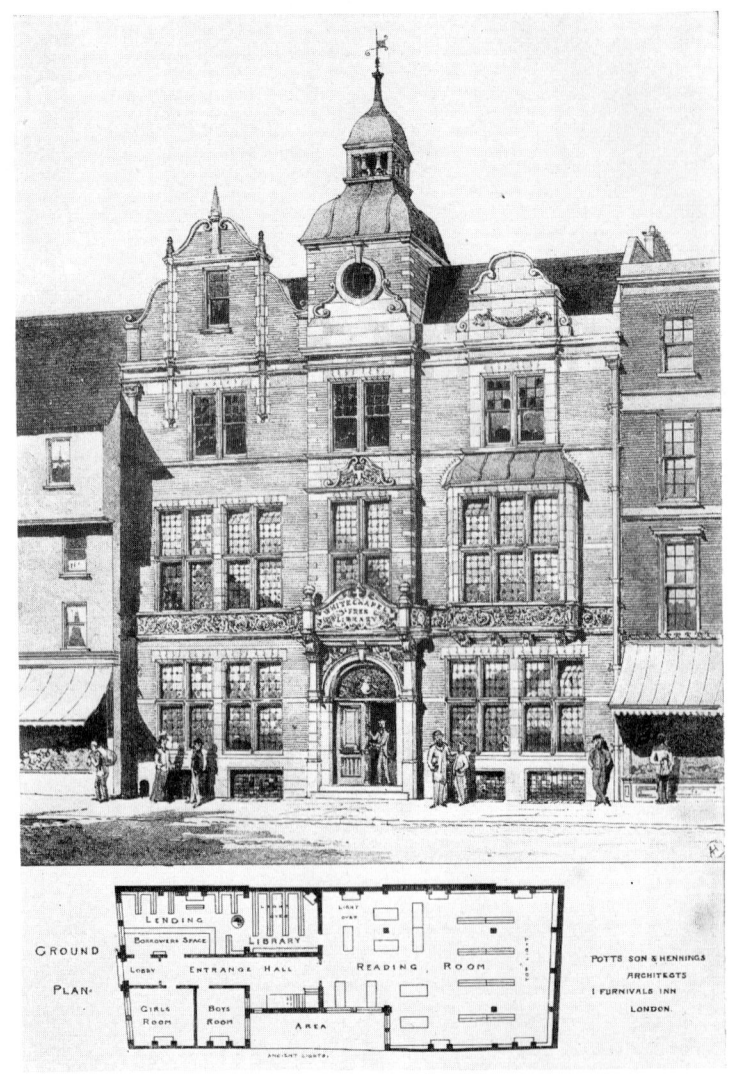

62

Above: The Haggerston Branch of Shoreditch Public Libraries at 236 Kingsland Road had two opening ceremonies, as, rather strangely for such a small building, it was constructed in two halves. The first half was opened on May 10th, 1893 by the Duke of Devonshire and the second early in 1897 by Sir Arthur Arnold, the then Chairman of the L.C.C. The building is no longer used for library purposes. This photograph is undated, but appears to be Edwardian. The first floor looks like a homely East London adaptation of the north front of the Old Ashmolean at Oxford. What, however, is one to make of the entrance? The curved pediment contrives to be both broken and open, while the detailing looks as if it might have come from S. Giorgio dei Greci in Venice. *Architect of the first section:* R. J. Lovell. *Architect of the second section:* Maurice Adams

Above: Edmonton Central Library was opened by Dr. Richard Garnett of the British Museum on November 20th, 1897. Richard Norman Shaw's First Alliance Assurance Building in Pall Mall seems a likely model, although here everything is naturally smaller and more domestic. The whole effect is unpretentious and very pleasing. The photograph is undated, but was taken about the time of the opening, as the houses under construction in the background date from this period. *Architect:* Maurice Adams

Above: St. George's in the East, Cable Street, Stepney, was opened on October 29th, 1898 by Lord Chief Justice Russell. The inspiration seems very strongly Richard Norman Shaw domestic. The Ipswich windows at first floor level were close in feel and treatment to those at Swan House on Chelsea Embankment or Shaw's own house at 6 Ellerdale Road, Hampstead, while the tall chimneys had a little of the appearance of the ones on the Kate Greenaway House at 39 Frognal, also in Hampstead. The rest of the façade, except for the entrance, used general detailing from private housing of the previous two decades. The entrance skipped lightly away from this pedestrian approach and was a frothy bit of Bavarian or Austrian Baroque, but with enough of the English stiff upper lip to prevent things going too far. The sketch is dated 1897 and was published in *Passmore Edwards Institutions* by J. J. Macdonald (Strand Newspaper Co., 1900). The building was demolished by bombing in the second world war. *Architect:* Maurice Adams

Above: Eltham Library, Woolwich, was opened on October 23rd, 1906 and the architect was Maurice Adams. This photograph is of 1914 and a water cart appears to have just gone round the corner. The central block looks as if it is a fairly close adaptation of the east front of the Old Ashmolean at Oxford. The deep triangular gables echo very strongly Philip Webb's Red House built for William Morris at nearby Bexley in 1859/60, while the four urns beside the gables also seem to be free adaptations from the Old Ashmolean. The rest of the structure has a domestic air, that could well go back to Adams' work at Bedford Park thirty years earlier. All in all, it sounds an unlikely combination, but in fact results in a very pleasing building

63

Above: This Library is situated in South Lambeth Road at the junction with Wilcox Road and is one of the strangest in Greater London. The main structure has more than a touch of the workhouse about it and is surmounted by two turrets, that end in something looking remarkably like the spiked helmets worn by Kaiser Bill's troops in the first world war. Note also the curious chimneys, which have the appearance of Brussels sprout stalks left in a field after the sprouts themselves have been picked. Most extraordinary was the semi-circular entrance with its caryatids and telamones, which was presumably designed to bring a touch of the 'warm South, Full of the true, the blushful Hippocrene' to the good citizens of Lambeth. It has, alas, been swept away in subsequent reconstruction work, no doubt because it was used as an unofficial loo by dogs and Saturday night drinkers. It was opened in early December 1888 by A. J. Mundella, M.P. This undated photograph appears to be of the 1920's, but the structure remains as it was first built. *Architect:* Sidney R. J. Smith

Above: This octagonal building was the first Minet Library in Knatchbull Road. William Minet had originally intended that it should be used as a meeting place for the tenants on his estate and also as a church hall for St. James, Knatchbull Road. However, on the death of his wife in 1887, he decided to turn the uncompleted building into a library in her memory. The contractor had by this time gone bankrupt and so a private company on co-operative lines was formed to complete the work. It was opened as a library in 1890, but was badly damaged by incendiary bombs in the second world war and has since been replaced. The photograph is undated, but appears to be Victorian. *Architect:* George Hubbard

Above: Not an aerial view of West Hill Library in Wandsworth, but one taken from the tower of the local fire station just before the first world war. The original three storey building on the left with the conservatory was opened in 1885 and the single storey Longstaff Reading Room (now the Reference Library) on the right was added at a later date. G. D. Longstaff was the first Chairman of the Wandsworth Library Commissioners. *Architects of the original building:* Smith & Gale. *Architect of the Longstaff Reading Room:* Ernest J. Elford

Above: Tottenham Central Library was opened on February 12th, 1896. The ground floor looks as if it had been designed for the London School Board, while the first floor is purely domestic. The building was originally symmetrical, but the section to the right of the right-hand gable was added at a later date (but soon after the opening), in place of a short length of blank wall corresponding to that on the left-hand side. More interestingly, the design is an almost exact copy of one section of Kilburn Library in Salusbury Road, except for slightly different pargetting on the gable. *Architects of both Tottenham and Kilburn Libraries:* Edmeston & Gabriel

Right: The Southwark Bridge Road Branch of Southwark Public Libraries (originally set up by St. Saviour's Parish) was opened on November 2nd, 1894, and this ceremony was to have been performed by the Prince of Wales. However, at the last moment he had to go into mourning because of the death of the Tsar and was not able to be present. The building, which ceased to be used as a library in November 1976, was described at the time of its construction as being of the 'English Renaissance Style', but this seems a gross over-simplification. The flattened arches of the ground floor are decidedly mannered and the rest of the façade is full of thin, nervous detailing. The strange tower seems to be a free adaptation of that on the now demolished St. John, Horsleydown, which stood at the southern approach to Tower Bridge. This supposition is strengthened by the fact that the Architect, John Johnson, also designed Bermondsey Library and would have known the church in question very well. The free-standing decorative feature in front of the tower is even stranger than the tower itself. The rectangular panel filled with Jacobean strap-work assumes the features of a frowning giant if observed closely, while the two supporting birds look as if they have drunk too much fire-water and, having slipped off an Indian totem pole, are just resting there until they feel strong enough to move again. This photograph was taken on July 5th, 1912. *Architect:* John Johnson

Below: The East Ham Library at Manor Park was opened on August 3rd, 1905 by James Bryce, M.P. It stands at the junction of Romford Road and Rabbits Road. This sturdily vulgar building seems to run through a great number of features from architectural pattern books, but probably at second rather than first hand. The Italian Mannerism of the ground floor appears to have come from somewhere like Richard Norman Shaw's Bryanston, while the general decoration looks more Arts and Crafts than Jacobean. The bust of Carnegie gazes down from its eyrie in the dated Dutch gable with a slightly bemused air, while the great names of literature in raised lettering, give way to the more homely 'Hovis Bread' and 'Cadbury's Chocolate' on the next door shop. The photograph is undated, but was probably taken soon after the opening. *Architect:* Adam Horsburgh Campbell

Above: Borough Road Library, Southwark, was opened on February 8th, 1899 by James Bryce, M.P. It has perhaps the most interesting example of Arts and Crafts and Art Nouveau decoration used on the elevation of any of the public libraries in Greater London. This sketch was published in *Passmore Edwards Institutions* by J. J. Macdonald (Strand Newspaper Co., 1900). One of the Architects, C. J. Phipps, was responsible for a number of West End theatres. *Architects:* C. J. Phipps and A. Bloomfield Jackson

Above and right: Modifications to buildings were often demanded by committees to cut costs. Both the Poplar Branch at Brunswick Road and the North Kensington Branch at the junction of Ladbroke Grove and Lancaster Road had a considerable amount of detailing removed before plans were finally approved. Particularly tragic was the loss of the tree of knowledge from the North Kensington Branch. Had this been executed, it would have been one of the first examples of exterior Art Nouveau decoration on a public building in England and ahead of Horta's work in Brussels. Brunswick Road Branch was opened on June 13th, 1906, the sketch of the original design coming from the *Building News* of January 15th, 1904. The photograph is of 1910. The North Kensington Branch was opened on October 29th, 1891 and the sketch of the tree of knowledge comes from the *Architect* of June 20th, 1890. *Architects of Brunswick Road Branch:* Squire, Myers & Petch

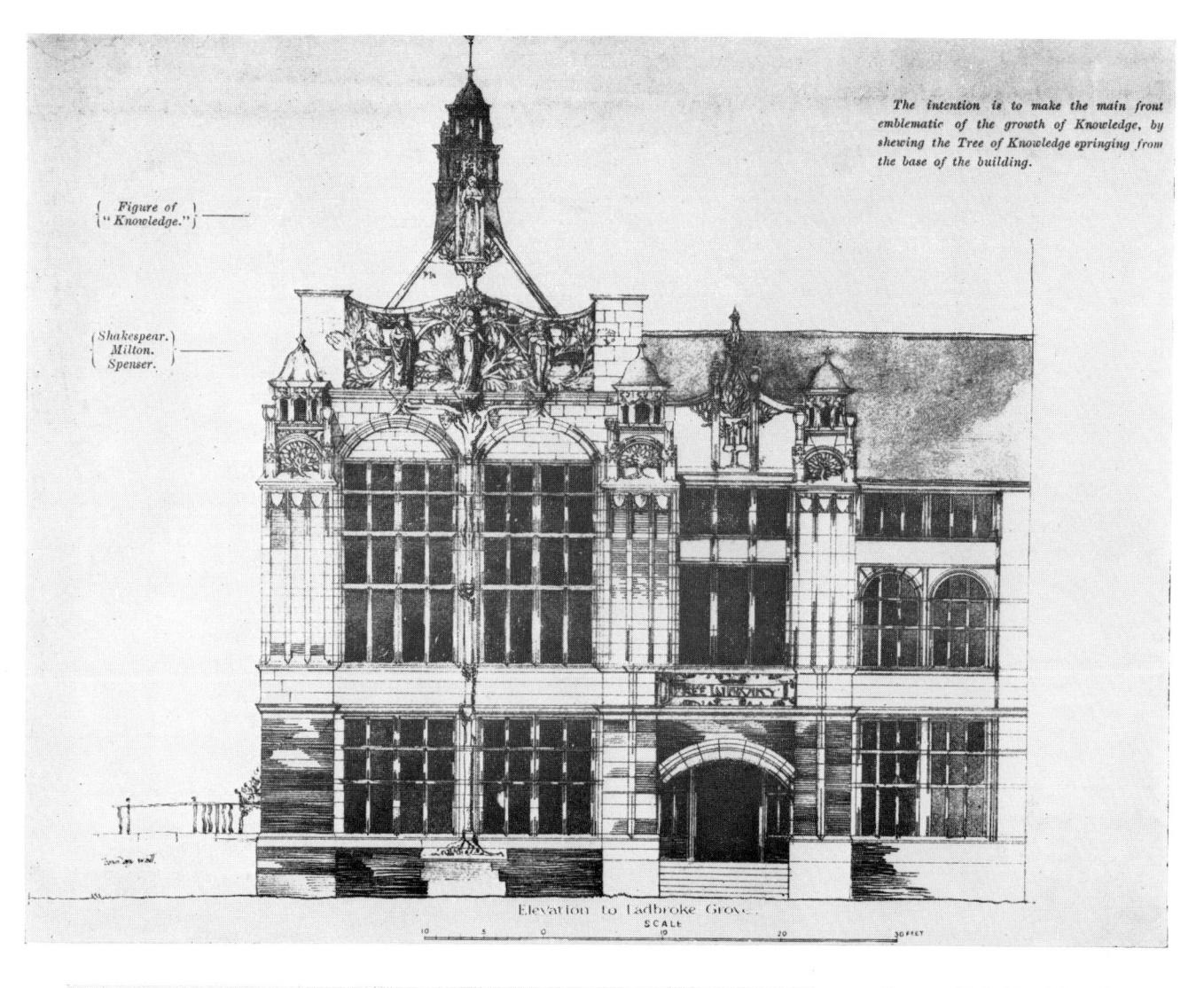

The intention is to make the main front emblematic of the growth of Knowledge, by shewing the Tree of Knowledge springing from the base of the building.

{ Figure of "Knowledge." }

{ Shakespear. Milton. Spenser. }

Elevation to Ladbroke Grove.

Above and left: North Kensington Branch. The photograph probably dates from early in the first world war. *Architects:* T. Phillips Figgis and H. Wilson

67

Left: This is the first public library to be encountered by a large number of foreign visitors to London. It is the Victoria Branch of the City of Westminster Public Libraries and stands in Buckingham Palace Road between the British Airways Terminal and Victoria Station. Rather like a white dwarf star, it is a highly compressed version of an early French Renaissance Chateau with a vast array of windows. The Library was opened on July 7th, 1894 and the photograph is of about that period. *Architect:* A. J. Bolton

Right: Woolwich Central Library was opened in William Street (since 1938, Calderwood Street) on November 8th, 1891 by Lord Avebury. The photograph is of 1914. The whole thing resembles nothing so much as a Victorian pub gone wrong. What is one to make of the long, thin windows on either side of the blown-up domestic bay window? Particularly unfortunate is the infilling on the left-hand doorway to produce an acceptable entrance for the flat at first floor level. The façade is completed by a monstrous chunk of Artisan Mannerist detailing, rather like the false fronts on some American small town buildings, which were designed to add a little tone to otherwise undistinguished edifices. *Architects:* Church, Quick and Whincop

Left: The Seven Kings Library in Ilford was opened on April 17th, 1909 and was the cause of some tart correspondence between Andrew Carnegie and the local authority. Ilford U.D.C. combined a rates office with the Library and hoped that Carnegie would pay for the whole building. You do not become a millionaire without handling situations of that kind swiftly and the U.D.C. were soon back-pedalling so fast, that they could hardly be seen for dust. The building seems a fairly long way after Richard Norman Shaw, which is appropriate, as it was designed by Henry Shaw, M.Inst.C.E., the local Surveyor. The main entrance is a large piece of Mannerism, which, with a little more imagination, could have incorporated a giant's face and open mouth in the style of the one at Bomarzo in the grounds of the Villa Orsini. Sadly, it must be allowed, that had this happened, the U.D.C. would never have passed the plans. The photograph was taken soon after the opening with the offending rates office forming an integral part of the building, but with its own entrance on the right in the side road (Blythswood Road). *Architect:* Henry Shaw

Above: Hammersmith Central Library was opened on July 24th, 1905 by the Duke of Argyll. The style is Edwardian Baroque, although with strong hints of the Mannerism, that was to be such a feature of Islington Central Library two years later. The centrally placed entrance and also the vaguely Michelangelesque figures between the ground and first floor windows at each end are certainly mannered in concept. The small statues of Shakespeare and Milton in niches at first floor level contrive to look thoroughly English and somewhat surprised to be in such exotic surroundings. From the *Building News*, May 20th, 1904. *Architect:* Henry T. Hare

Below: Islington Central Library was opened on October 24th, 1907. It is possibly the best example of Edwardian Mannerism of any library in Greater London. The three open pediments have large scroll work plaques leading to brackets surmounted by classical heads. Between these brackets and heads are blank circular window openings with surrounds, the whole joined by swags of fruit and flowers. It is perhaps not surprising that the two statues of Bacon and Spenser in niches face slightly outwards and away from this extraordinary detailing. The entrance seems to be a free rendering of that of Morden College, Blackheath, with the exception of the prominent keystone, which is copied from the one at St. Helen's, Bishopsgate. From the *Builder*, February 1st, 1908. *Architect:* Henry T. Hare

Left: If this building had ever been constructed, it might best have been described as Edwardian Hellenistic, with the eccentrically placed tower-cum-turret balancing the equally eccentrically conceived entrance. It was placed third in the list of submitted designs for Islington Central Library and, shorn of its decoration, looks like the father and mother of all gas and electricity showrooms. Hare's successful design looks highly conservative when placed beside it. From the *Architectural Review*, Volume 18, 1905, page 249. *Architect:* Beresford Pite

Right: This modest villa was the Belsize Branch of Hampstead Public Libraries from its opening on April 10th, 1897 until it had to be closed as an unsafe structure in 1936. It was situated in Antrim Road and the present building, which replaced it in 1937, was constructed on the same site. *Architect of the original building:* Charles H. Lowe, Surveyor to the Hampstead Vestry

Left: This plain, unvarnished outpost of Empire is the Stoke Newington Central Library dressed overall for the coronation of George V on June 22nd, 1911. There is a photograph of the King in the third window from the left on the ground floor. The flat at first floor level is apparent from the curtaining. The roof turret with its large union jack looks like something out of a film set, with a Gatling gunner about to appear and mow down hordes of extras tricked out as advancing Zulus. The building was opened on July 23rd, 1892 by John Passmore Edwards and the ivy had obviously grown extremely vigorously in the nineteen years before this photograph was taken. *Architects:* Bridgman and Goss

Right: The site of Hackney Central Library before the present building was constructed. An undated photograph, but probably Edwardian. The horse is being led into a smithy with the somewhat improbable wording 'Corby Child's Veterinary Forge and Infirmary' above the door

Below: The site itself is an awkward shape at the junction of Mare Street and Paragon Road and the architect solved the problem neatly with a straightforward piece of Edwardian Baroque. The building was opened on May 28th, 1908 and still serves as Hackney Central Library. From the *Builder,* March 24th, 1906. *Architect:* H. A. Crouch

Below: The Hackney solution was not lost on the architects, who were successful in the competition for the St. Pancras Central Library on a very similar site. Details of their design appeared in the architectural press in July and August 1906 only four months after those for Hackney in March of the same year. Although the interior layouts were different, the elevations were very similar examples of Edwardian Baroque. The St. Pancras Central Library was to be sited at the junction of Prince of Wales Road and Grafton Yard, but was never built. From the *British Architect,* August 24th, 1906. *Architects:* S. B. Russell and T. Edwin Cooper

Living on the Job

Sometimes a flat was provided for a Chief's use and this was generally above or beside the library itself. A separate entrance was normal although, in addition, there was often one of those circular iron staircases, now so beloved of trendy interior decorators, pirouetting its way down through the ceiling of one of the library departments.

Heating and lighting were frequently provided at cheap rates, and some mean Chiefs diverted library cleaning materials for their own use. One even went to the lengths of marking toilet paper with cabalistic signs in a lavatory, which lay in a kind of no-man's land between his flat and the library proper, in an effort to detect illegal use of this much sought-after facility.

A Chief's wife had to be treated with circumspection, as she could act as a kind of copper's nark and report on the late arrival of staff. A Chief living on the job often found time to read large quantities of periodicals and these had to be ready on the dot. The unfortunate junior assistant told off to do this job was placed in the untenable middle ground between the erratic supply system of a local newsagent and the wrath of the Chief.

Flats were occasionally also provided for caretakers, either under the eaves or in the basement, on the analogy of servants' quarters in large country houses. Presumably accommodation for either Chiefs or caretakers had a degree of enlightened self-interest on the part of municipal authorities, as the best fire alarm system yet designed is the swiftness of human reaction to a rapidly increasing warmth in the soles of one's feet.

Below: Battersea Central Library, Lavender Hill, at the junction with Lavender Sweep. Note the children at the window of the flat at first floor level. The building is in a neo-Dutch style and was opened in 1890. It was extended in the 1930's. An undated photograph, which appears to be Victorian. *Architect:* E. W. Mountford.

Above: Erith Central Library was opened on April 7th, 1906. Much fascinating detail about its construction has survived. At one point an extra £45 was voted 'to opalite the sanitary conveniences' and this was followed by an agreement that '1d in the slot fastenings should be fixed to the doors'. At one stage the Committee authorised that 'hot water service and copper be provided in the Librarian's rooms'. In the photograph, taken about the time of the opening, these latter can be seen clearly at first floor level. The round port-hole windows give a faint echo of ocean-going liners and the jaunty turret and spire emphasise this nautical analogy. The nearness of the shipping lanes in the Thames Estuary must have made these architectural features seem very appropriate in an otherwise plain and straightforward building. *Architect:* W. Egerton

Furniture and Fittings

Solidity was the watchword of the designers of early public library furniture. For reference or reading room tables, newspaper slopes and book issue counters, oak was the preferred wood, although walnut and mahogany were also used. Before specialist library suppliers became common, the architect of a library was often asked to design the furniture and fittings as well. At the turn of the century a good deal of Art Nouveau design went into library fittings, much of which has been swept away since by subsequent interior modifications.

It is intriguing to see the same arguments being advanced today about the relative merits of wooden or steel shelving, that were current before the first world war. Wooden shelving if not dark when new, rapidly darkened with age and when filled with rebound books, gave a sombre appearance, which was intended to induce a hushed and respectful approach by readers.

Steel shelving on the other hand had a rather brash air of spartan efficiency and although some designs had splendid curvilinear decoration on the upright endpieces, the majority tended to be stark and angular.

On the analogy that you could have any colour in a Ford car as long as it was black, metal shelving came in an equally wide spectrum, as long as it was khaki. Although a public library with wooden shelving was clearly a secular building, it had a faintly ecclesiastical air, somewhat more Nonconformist than Anglican, whereas rows of steel shelving on the other hand produced an atmosphere reminiscent of the stores section of an engineering factory.

Although time has produced some actual variation in the colour of metal shelving and there are now combinations of metal and wood, librarians in the 1970's still tend to show a marked preference for one material or the other, without being able to give any very logical reasons for why this is so.

Periodical and newspaper stands provided designers with the chance to indulge in delightful flights of individual fancy and many of their creations were sculptural objects in their own right. This exuberance was also allowed free rein in the decorated surrounds of indicators and some had Elizabethan strap-work that would not have looked out of place in Hardwick Hall.

Above: The idea of water sprites appealed immensely to artistic sensibilities during the Art Nouveau period and in 1888 there was a particularly influential translation of Delamotte Fouqué's *Undine*, illustrated by Heywood Sumner. At the North Kensington Branch (see page 67), an attempt to have a tree of knowledge as part of the exterior design was defeated because of costs, but this fireplace was constructed and it bears a close resemblance to Sumner's cover for the 1888 translation of *Undine*. The sketch is No. 757 by T. Raffles Davison from the Arts and Crafts Exhibition, No. 3, 1890

Above: A fireplace from the Minet Library in Knatchbull Road, Lambeth. This photograph must date from before the opening in 1890, as the fireplace is still under construction. It was a casualty of the second world war and destroyed in an incendiary raid on the building

Below: The Jacobean style staircase of Walthamstow Central Library. The photograph appears to have been taken about the time of the opening on July 10th, 1909

Below: At the sale of Horace Walpole's house at Strawberry Hill, Twickenham, a quantity of the stained glass was bought by Sir John Philippart and some of this was later acquired by C. H. Bennett of College House, Hammersmith. After his death, some eighty pieces of the glass were presented by his widow to Hammersmith Borough Council in 1911 and placed in the Central Library. Some of the glass is Victorian, but there is also a good selection of Flemish or possibly Dutch work. This example is a small piece of what appears to be Flemish armorial glass

Above: Waldegrave Road Library, Teddington, was opened on April 11th, 1906. This photograph of the lending library was also taken in 1906. Observe the decorated metal shelving and the desk that looks like something out of a sub-post office. *Architect:* Henry Cheers

Right: The spiral staircase at Clerkenwell (later Finsbury) Central Library. It went from the ground floor to the top of the building. The photograph is of 1967, just before the demolition of the building, but the staircase was part of the original structure of 1890

Below: End elevation and sections of newsroom slopes and reference library tables, taken from blueprints for furniture in Erith Central Library. The blueprints are undated, but were prepared for firms, which wished to tender in January 1906. As the Library was opened on April 7th, 1906, the work had to be executed quickly

Right: The estimate of the successful firm, The Library Supply Company

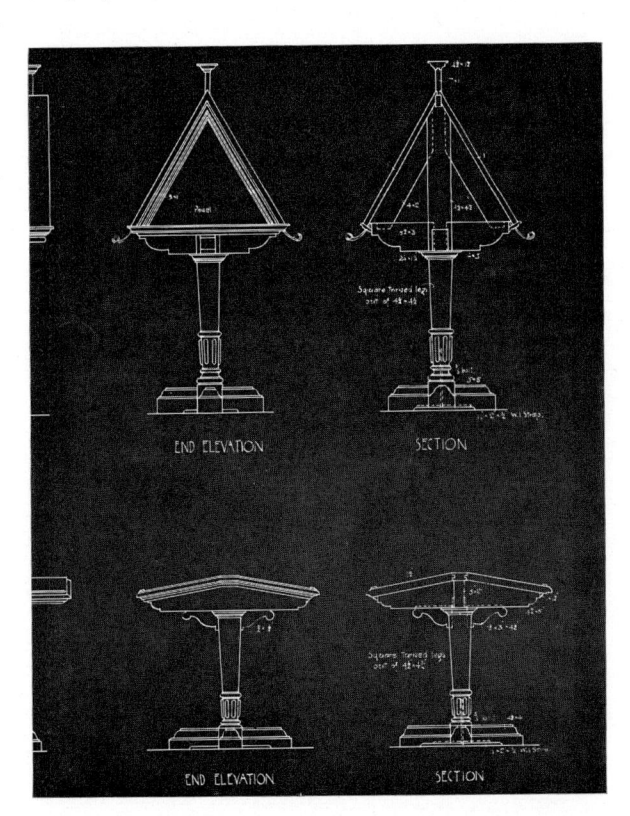

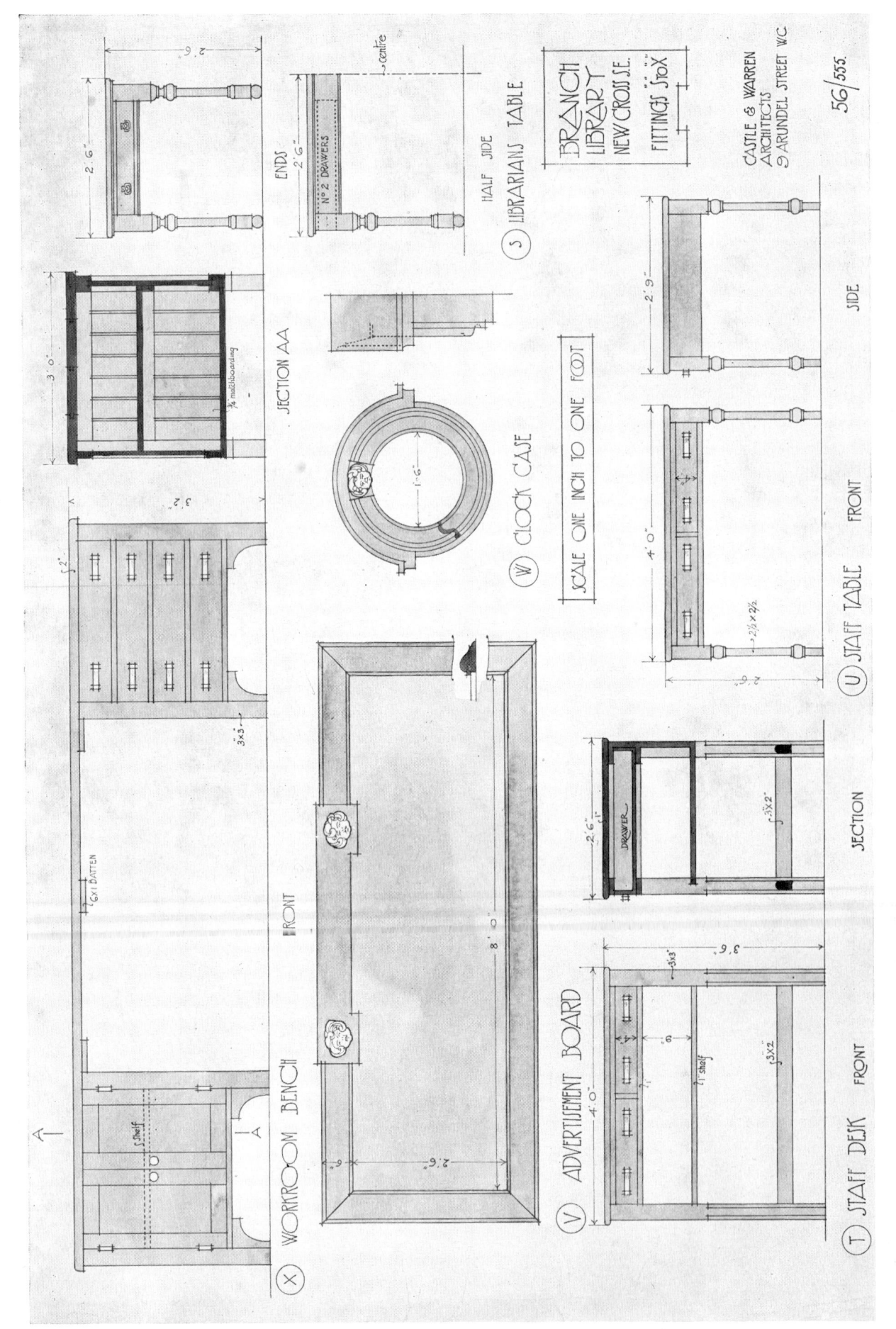

Above: Architect's drawings for the furniture and fittings of the New Cross Branch of Deptford Public Libraries. The Branch was opened on July 24th, 1911 and these undated drawings must have been produced late in 1910 or early 1911. *Architects*: Castle and Warren

Lighting, Heating and Ventilation

While electric lighting had become general in most town libraries by the end of the first decade of the twentieth century, it had been preceded by what now seem a bewildering variety of alternatives. Light could be obtained from coal gas or acetylene gas, the latter productive of an overpowering smell, if there was the slightest leak. Outside towns, petroleum or alcohol lamps had their advocates, while town gas could be used in gas engines to produce electricity.

These alternatives to mains electricity were all productive of dirt, soot or dampness, which were obviously injurious to books. Nobody seemed particularly worried if they were also harmful to the staff and public.

In the provision of heating and ventilation, architects were acutely aware, that if they provided the former, there was the utmost incentive to install the latter on a generous scale. The newsroom was of course the centre of the problem and phrases such as 'the unwashed' or 'malodorous idlers' abounded when the subject came under discussion.

The most common form of heating was a low-pressure hot water system with its radiators and intestinal windings of black pipes. Ventilation was ideally by mechanical or electrical extractors, but it was an art obviously very much in its infancy and building committees had a tendency to latch on to this as a rather namby-pamby provision, that if not omitted completely, could be reduced to the point of almost total ineffectiveness. In this unhappy, but all too familiar situation, the only hope was high ceilings, large windows and a strong east wind.

Above: Two examples of gas lighting. The undated photograph on the left is of Stoke Newington Central Library, presumably soon after its opening on July 23rd, 1892. On the right, the photograph of the newsroom and reference library at Clerkenwell is also undated, but as the building was opened on October 10th, 1890, it seems reasonable from its appearance to assume a date in the 1890's. Even for the period, it is certainly very rough and ready and resembles one of those mission halls, which were such features of the revivalist life of the times. The pictures on the end wall have the air of religious oleographs of great moral uplift, but minimal artistic taste

Right: Walthamstow Central Library was opened on July 10th, 1909 and has a great deal of interesting Art Nouveau detailing. Particularly noteworthy are these elegant light fitments in the reference library. The photograph is undated, but before 1920, as the room remained unaltered between the opening and that date. Behind the plunging statue lurks a particularly good example of a radiator

Lending Libraries

May 1st, 1894 saw the opening of the first properly safeguarded open-access library in this country at the now demolished flat-iron building, which was the former Finsbury Central Library up to 1967. From 1894 until the first world war, the whole management of lending libraries was a battle between open-access and the indicator, which had hitherto reigned supreme since its first installation at Manchester in 1863.

The two main protagonists were J. D. Brown for open-access and Alfred Cotgreave for the indicator. Brown was Librarian of Finsbury and, after 1905, of Islington until his death in 1914. Cotgreave, who held posts at Wednesbury, Richmond, Wandsworth and West Ham, combined these with the patenting and sale of indicators and other library fittings.

The whole controversy was conducted with great bitterness and although to librarians practising in the 1970's, it may seem all to have happened a long time ago, the battle marked a turning point in British librarianship. For the first time, ordinary readers were allowed to browse among an extensive collection of books, something which up till then had been the prerogative of a very small segment of the population.

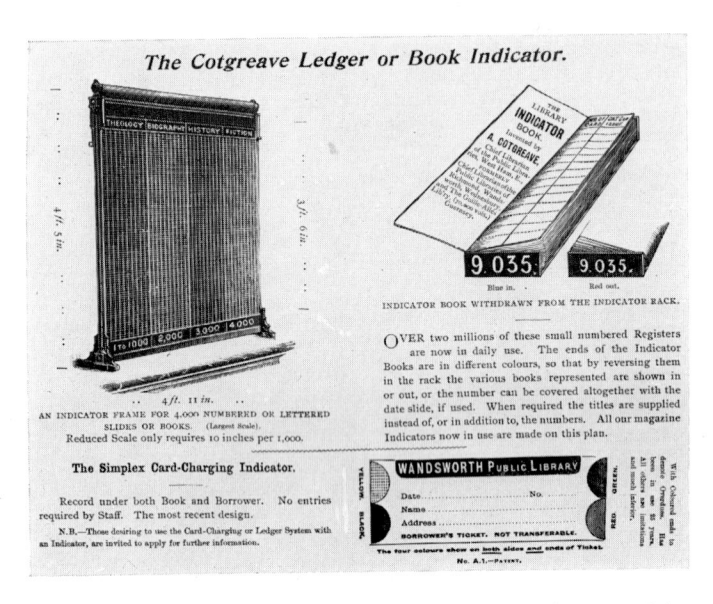

Above: Advertising material for Cotgreave's Indicator explaining how it was used. Until a few years ago, the same system with slight modifications known as the Cotgreave Cask Recording Indicator was used by breweries to keep track of their deliveries

Below: Two views of indicators. That on the left is at the Victoria Branch of Westminster Public Libraries, where closed access survived until 1931. The photograph is undated and could be any time up to 1931. However, the lettering on the notice about the catalogue and the ghostly lighting fitments have an Edwardian air about them. On the right is a photograph of the Hammersmith Central Library indicator taken in 1906, a year after the building was opened

Above: Two indicator tickets, that have survived. The Poplar example is one of the Cotgreave type, while the one from Richmond has no maker's name. The latter was returned to Richmond from the effects of a lady of over ninety, who died very recently. It must be one of the earliest surviving public library tickets in this country

Above: Four more views of indicators. At the top left is the Livesey Library, Camberwell, in about 1907. At the top right is Enfield Central Library in August 1912 and at the bottom left Walthamstow Central Library in about 1910, a year or so after it was opened. The photograph at the bottom right is Brunswick Road Library, Poplar, about 1912. The two figures are the then Branch Librarian, William Benson Thorne and his daughter, Winifred. Benson Thorne was later to become Librarian of Poplar from 1934 to 1942

Below: No lending library was complete without a battery of notices. One appears on the previous page, two here and more at the bottom of the next page. All are from Richmond Public Libraries

NOTICE *re* HOLIDAYS.

The Library will be closed (under rule 3) on Christmas Day. On Boxing Day the News-Room only will be open.

By Order of the Library Committee,

ALBERT A. BARKAS,

Librarian and Secretary.

Books Due Back on Monday, December 25th and Tuesday, December 26th | may be returned on Wednesday, December 27th free of fines.

Richmond Public Library.
LENDING DEPARTMENT.

RESERVATION OF BOOKS.

UPON payment of ONE PENNY any Book will be RESERVED, and a Notice sent to the Borrower immediately it is available. The Book must be called for within Twenty-four Hours of the receipt of the Notice, otherwise it will be again put into circulation.

Broad and Co., Printers, 8, King Street, Richmond.

Above: Open-access started at Clerkenwell on May 1st, 1894 and this undated photograph appears to have been taken soon after this date. The shelving looks as if it had hardly been changed much from the days of the indicator and the reach of a gorilla would have been an advantage to readers wishing to savour the delights of high rise literature

Right: The wicket, by which readers were only admitted to a library, if the staff released the gate. This was an essential part of the concept of 'safeguarded' open-access

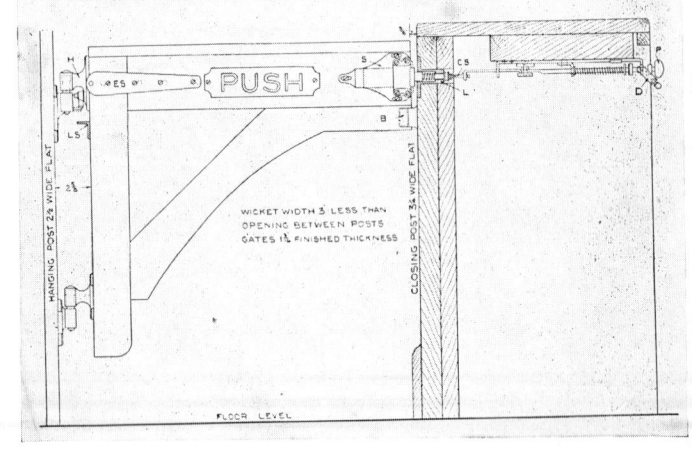

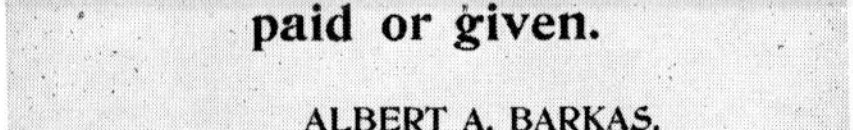

Above: St. George's in the East Library in Cable Street, Stepney, opened on October 29th, 1898 and possessed this pioneer library for the blind with braille and moon scripts. The photograph is undated, but appears to be Edwardian. The building was destroyed by bombing in the second world war

LAMBERT PASSIMETER WICKET FITTINGS

Left and below: You have been warned

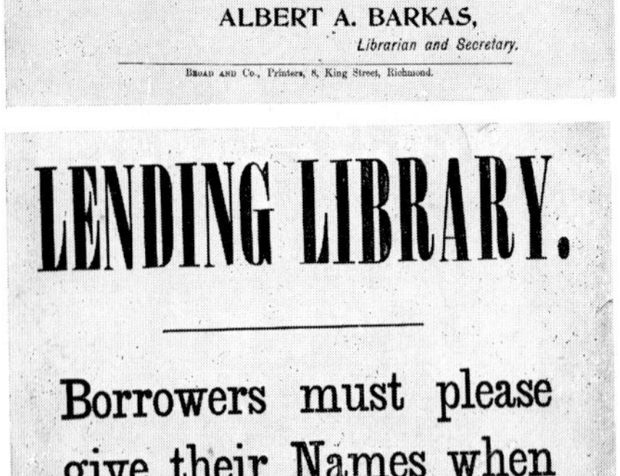

Receipts for Fines &c.

Borrowers are requested to see that they get Receipts for all Moneys paid or given.

ALBERT A. BARKAS,
Librarian and Secretary.

LENDING LIBRARY.

Borrowers must please give their Names when Changing Books.

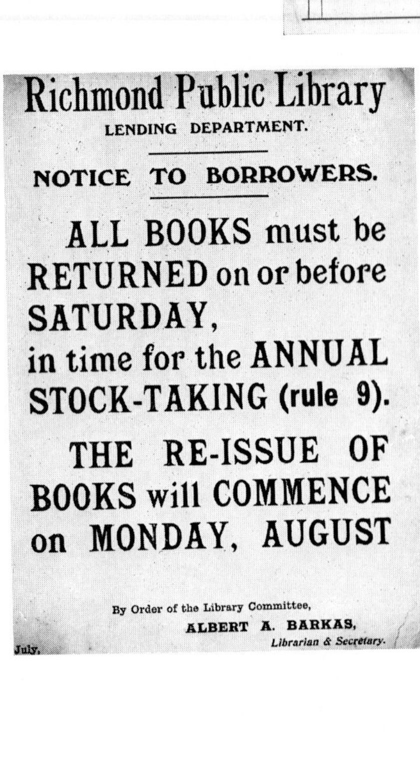

Richmond Public Library
LENDING DEPARTMENT.

NOTICE TO BORROWERS.

ALL BOOKS must be RETURNED on or before SATURDAY, in time for the ANNUAL STOCK-TAKING (rule 9).

THE RE-ISSUE OF BOOKS will COMMENCE on MONDAY, AUGUST

By Order of the Library Committee,
ALBERT A. BARKAS,
Librarian & Secretary.

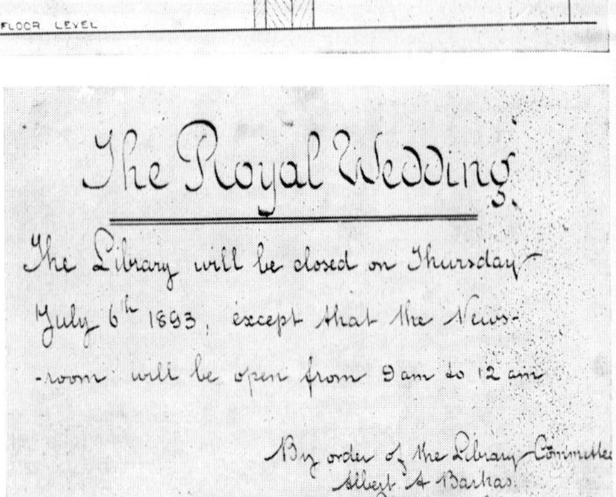

The Royal Wedding

The Library will be closed on Thursday July 6th 1893, except that the News-room will be open from 9am to 12am

By order of the Library Committee
Albert A. Barkas
Librarian & Secretary

NO DOGS ADMITTED.

Reference Libraries

Reference libraries gave the public library movement a chance to put on some intellectual muscle and their design reflected this ambition. Many were an amalgam of features from libraries in large country houses and Oxbridge colleges, with something of the King's Library in the British Museum thrown in for good measure.

Shelving often went up to just under ceiling level and the highest books could only be reached with the aid of ladders. Notices were attached to them disclaiming responsibility for accidents, a very necessary precaution on the part of the local authority, as many years of use rendered them highly dangerous, if not handled correctly. Some people from long practice could shin up like alpinists, but staff tended to hover around new readers essaying their first climb, with the anxious look of ski-instructors taking novices up to the nursery slopes for preliminary training.

A more spacious air could be created by the addition of a gallery, although if this were done in an area that was not large enough, it created nothing more than a rather miserable cat-walk with hardly enough room for two people to pass. All in all, an atmosphere of scholarship was the desired end, to offset those light romances, westerns and thrillers in the lending department and for many Chiefs the sight of so much studious enquiry being so diligently pursued, had an ego-massaging and therapeutic value out of all proportion to what was being actually achieved.

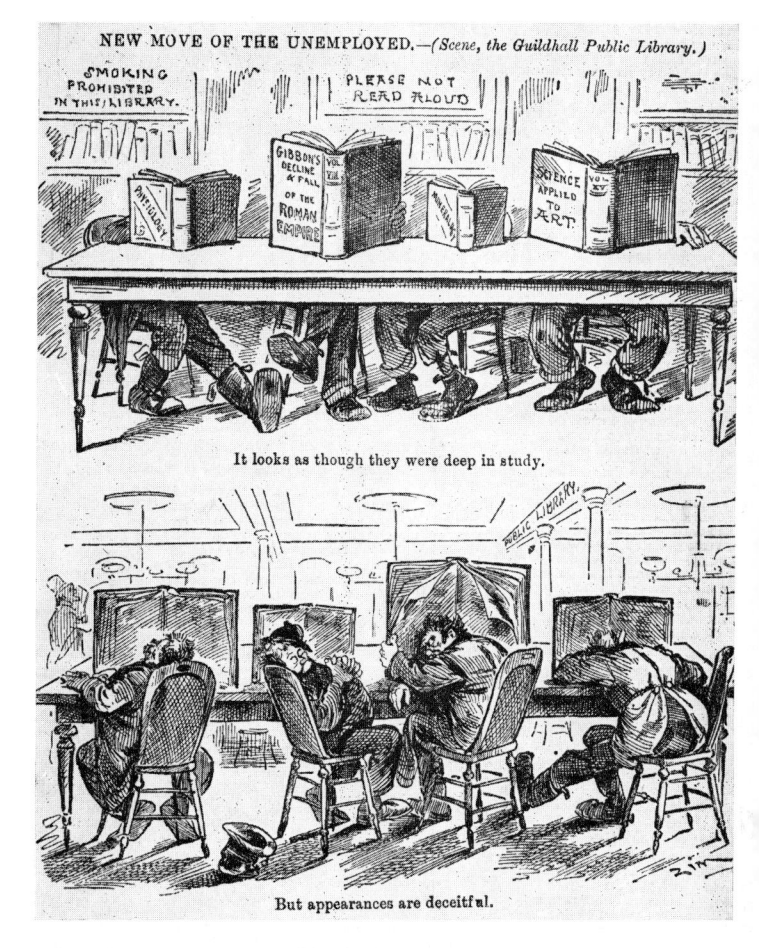

Above: Layabouts in the Guildhall Library. From the periodical *Illustrated Bits* of March 28th, 1885. Gibbon's *Decline and Fall of the Roman Empire* naturally provides more shade and protection than the work entitled *Mineralogy*

Below: On the left is an undated, but probably Edwardian photograph of the Victoria Library in Buckingham Palace Road, Westminster. On the right is the Southwark Central Reference Library in 1905. Both have narrow galleries, while the Southwark ladder is a fine example of its kind. Also the busts and portrait that could be Passmore Edwards, Tolstoy or Elijah are typical of the period. *Architect of Southwark Central Library:* l'Anson

> **O Rest in the Lord**
> **Mendelssohn**
>
> Caution. The Original Manuscript Score by the Composer of the above Air from the Oratorio of Elijah, and an Autograph Letter from him to Mr Bartholomew dated May 28th 1846 recently presented to the Guildhall Library by Mrs Mounsey Bartholomew are missing therefrom.
>
> Any information tending to their recovery should be addressed to the Librarian. In the event of either of these Manuscripts being offered for sale, the public are hereby informed that they are the property of the Corporation of London by whom they are claimed.
>
> Guildhall, E.C.
> May 1880

Above left: This cartoon by an unidentified hand is of borrowers and staff in the Guildhall Library in 1885

Above: Theft has always been a problem in reference libraries and this is a particularly spectacular example

Left: The Guildhall Library. A sketch from the *Illustrated London News* of November 9th, 1872. A fine example of reproduction East Anglian Perpendicular. The Guildhall Library moved to its present new premises in 1974. *Architect of the still existing 1872 building:* Sir Horace Jones

Below: Woolwich Central Reference Library. An excellent example of an imitation Later Medieval Domestic arch-braced collar beam roof. The tables are Edwardian Jacobean and the catalogue early standard Libraco. There is also an interesting line in decorated radiators. The photograph was taken in 1914

Above: An undated photograph of Hampstead Central Reference Library, which looks as if it were taken in the Edwardian period. On view is a pseudo hammer beam roof with tie beams in the Renaissance manner, backed by a circular extraction fan, an interesting if somewhat exotic combination. Note the cat walk to the upper book shelves and the double catalogue drawers on the extreme left. These were inordinately heavy and if handled unwarily, could precipitate their entire and considerable contents on the floor

Below: Putting on the dog. West Ham Central Reference Library at the junction of Romford Road and Water Lane. One of a series of photographs taken for the opening in 1898. Mottoes round the dome, marble pillars and a handsome bookcase make this one of the best fitted-out libraries of the period

Above right: Tonks' shelf fitting. Known by generations of librarians, especially when a handful of books placed on a shelf made it collapse instantly, because only two or three out of the four necessary fittings were actually in position

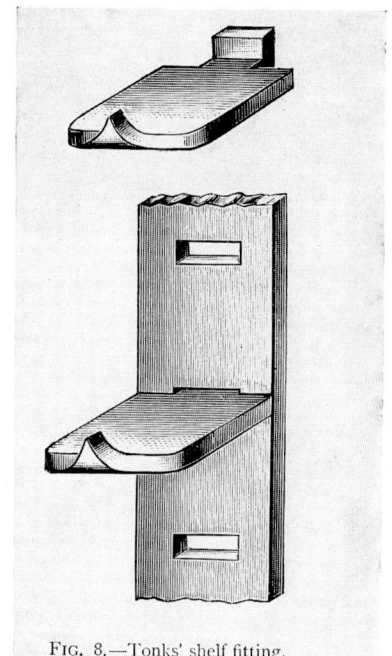

FIG. 8.—Tonks' shelf fitting.

Below right: Cotgreave's No. 1 step. This murderous device was fitted to high shelving. You leapt for a grab handle and put your foot on the step at the same time. If you were not very careful, it caught you a paralysing blow on the shin. If your foot slipped off it without actual damage, you were left hanging from the grab handle like a stranded orang-utan

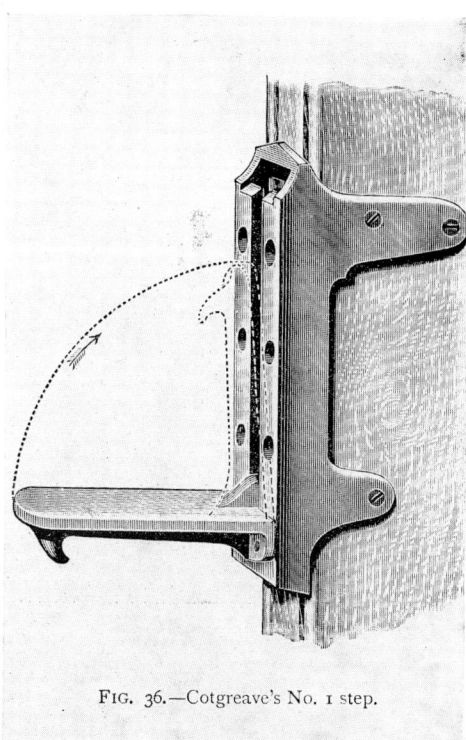

FIG. 36.—Cotgreave's No. 1 step.

83

Children's Libraries

Provision for the needs of children in early buildings was either non-existent or left a great deal to be desired. Basements were considered highly suitable, because most use would be made of the facilities in the winter after school hours. Although attempts were occasionally made to provide separate accommodation for boys and girls, and sometimes even a mirroring of the services for adults, by junior reference or newsrooms as well as lending libraries, the premium on space prevented this from becoming general.

In keeping with the spirit of the age, formality was the keynote and a fairly strict control was kept on what children were permitted to do. However, within these somewhat forbidding confines, a great deal of pioneering work was carried out and a host of people had an interest in reading awakened in an atmosphere, that may have lacked the light and colour of later years, but was certainly not short of dedication on the part of the library staff.

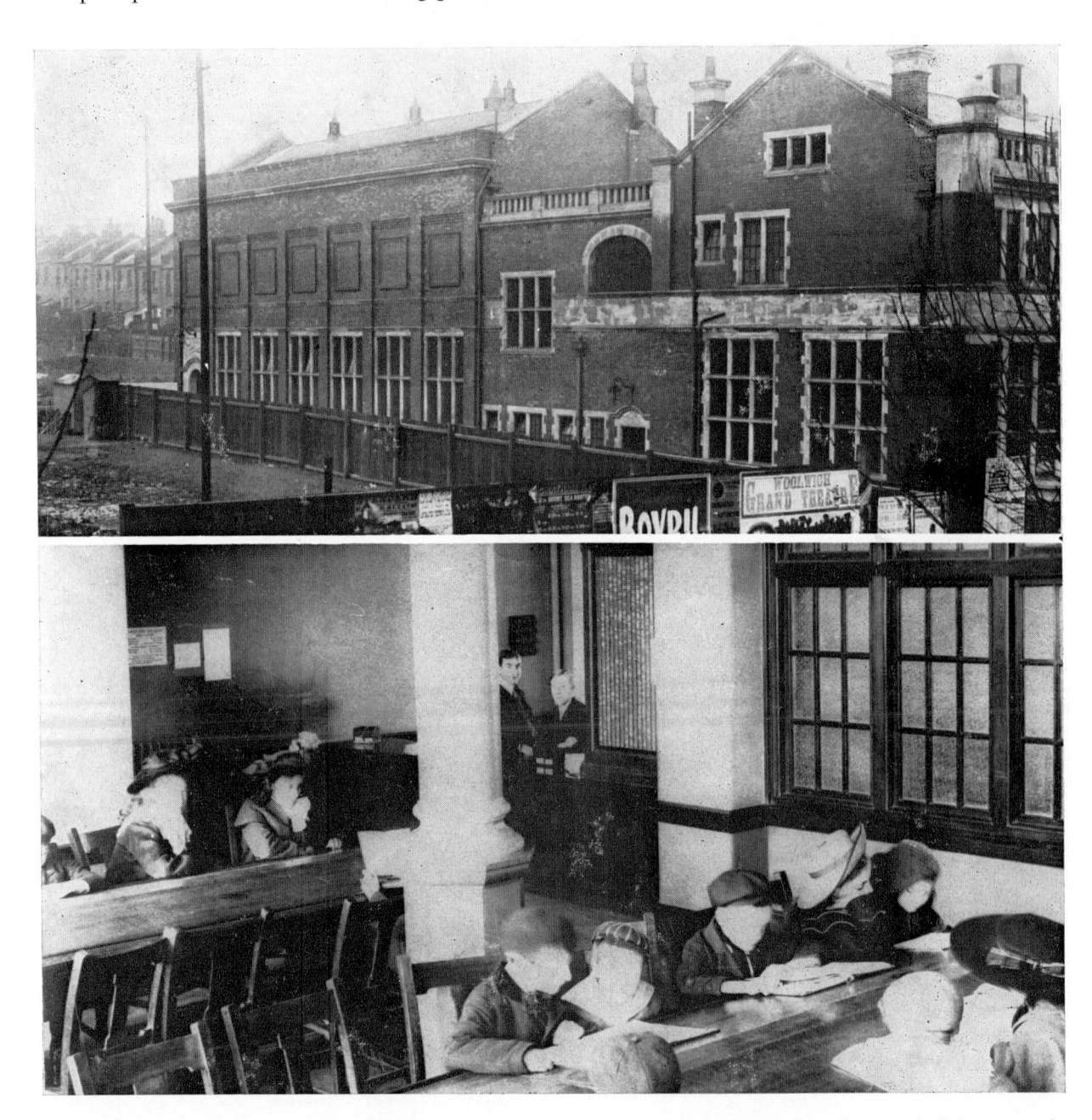

Above: Exterior and interior views of the Plumstead Children's Library. Both were taken in 1904. In the exterior view, the Children's Library is the section of the building at the far left with its own entrance. The department had its own indicator, although small children would have needed very well developed eyesight to have made any use of the top half. It seems to be run by that slave labour, which masquerades as 'junior readers being allowed to help'. *Architect:* Frank Sumner, Borough Engineer and Surveyor

Newsrooms

When public library building started in earnest during the 1880's in London, architects were encouraged, as in the rest of the urban areas of the country, to provide generous accommodation for the reading of newspapers and periodicals, which were often segregated into separate rooms. Yet a third room was sometimes provided for ladies, ostensibly to cater for reading matter thought likely to appeal particularly to the feminine mind, but more importantly to protect them from the denizens of the other two rooms.

Every urban librarian up to at least the 1960's, could produce a personal horror story about a newsroom, and although many of these had been embroidered in the telling, they were based on a rock-solid core of experience. Because newsrooms were warm and free, they offered the perfect haven for tramps, layabouts and the passers of betting slips. The weary could find repose, the loquacious hold furtive conversations about the iniquity of authority generally and the brash jeer at the staff. Any ordinary members of the public, who genuinely sought information from the available reading matter, were forced to pick their way delicately around these various obstructions.

Chief librarians and caretakers fought a running battle to maintain order in this potential anarchy, calling upon the bye-laws and in extreme cases, the police. The average constable was not interested in anything short of grievous bodily harm and the bye-laws were a flimsy ally for a junior assistant faced with a menacing tough. A copy of *Crockford's Clerical Dictionary* or *Burke's Peerage* dropped from a foot high close to a sleeping tramp could work wonders, especially as it might be justified vaguely as tidying up. While the palpitating victim gathered the remnants of his nerves together, all the windows were then flung open on the pretext of clearing the air. If the victim then slunk out, it was as well to watch him closely, as his usual riposte was to relieve himself down the back stairs.

Apart from the solidity of the furniture, the abiding memory of newsrooms was the smell. The zoological aroma brought forth by an April morning just after a heavy shower had ensured a packed congregation of regulars, was one that was not soon forgotten.

Above: For those who think that *Judy* was merely a library furniture maker's idea of a joke, it may be of interest to know, that it was an actual periodical subtitled *The London Serio-Comic Journal*, which flourished from 1867 to 1907. This piece of furniture was produced by the Library Bureau

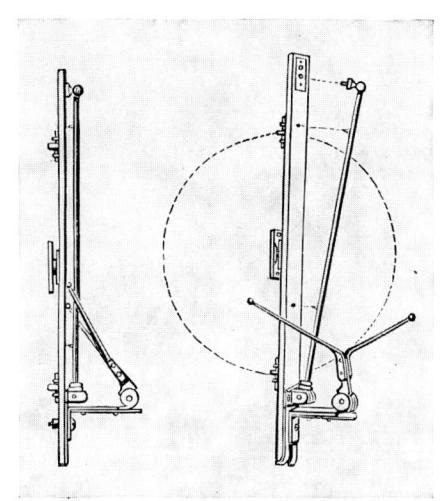

Above: The Heathcote revolving illustrated newspaper-holder, or the invention that made the newsroom possible. Trying to put a newspaper onto this device was like doing battle with an unfriendly octopus
Left and below: Two types of magazine rack from the fertile brain of Alfred Cotgreave. The table model gives the curious impression of actually walking towards you with mincing steps

Above: A cartoon from the *Lady's Pictorial* of April 20th, 1895, mostly concerned with ladies at Kensington Central Library monopolising periodicals. The laboured approach to humour is very noticeable

Above right: The newsroom of the Victoria Library, Buckingham Palace Road, Westminster, with splendid light fitments like plunging sea-horses. An undated photograph, but thought to be Edwardian

Right: Further examples of notices from Richmond Public Libraries

Below: Putney newsroom about 1900. The newspaper stands resemble lecterns and the whole room has an ecclesiastical appearance. One can almost imagine a low church lesson-reading competition for the laity, with adjudicators about to take their places at the tables on the left. The light fitments have outstanding examples of municipal crinkle-crankle glass shades. Architect: F. J. Smith

CONVERSATION NOT ALLOWED.

Readers when moving about the Room are requested to do so as quietly as possible.

FREE PUBLIC LIBRARY, RICHMOND.

Readers are cautioned against losing sight of their Umbrellas or Handbags, as the Officials cannot be held responsible for their safety.

NOTICE. £1 REWARD

The Library Committee regrets to find that on several occasions Newspapers and Magazines have been mutilated or stolen. The assistance of the public is invited in preventing this abuse of the Library; and the above Reward will be paid to any one affording such information as shall lead to the conviction of any offender.

By Order of the Library Committee,
ALBERT A. BARKAS,
Secretary and Librarian.

THE FREE PUBLIC LIBRARY

Faces the Little Green and is close to the Railway Station.

THE READING ROOM contains a liberal selection of the important Daily and Weekly Newspapers, Periodicals, & Monthly Magazines.

Above: Balham Library Newsroom in 1898. The area was once famous for the number of actors who lived there, many of whom were 'resting' at any given moment. The gentleman on the extreme right of the photograph looks as if he might well have fallen into that category. More importantly, the two objects, which appear to be handles on the ends of each of the nearest tables with the curious troughs and cross bars beneath them, are receptacles for wet umbrellas. These are part of the standard equipment of all Nonconformist conventicles of the period, as going by public transport to a service was considered sinful in the extreme. If the congregation had beaten its way to worship through a rainstorm, drops of water trickled slowly down an impressive array of umbrellas, making little tinkling noises in the iron troughs on the floor at the end of each pew. They appear to have been provided only infrequently in newsrooms, perhaps just another example of discouraging the long-stay clientele. *Architect:* Sidney R. J. Smith

Below: Lurline Gardens Branch, Battersea. This photograph of the newsroom was taken about 1900. Note that *Church Bells* rubs shoulders with *Labour Gazette* and *Queen* with *Work*. On the far left emigration to Canada, Australia and New Zealand is being encouraged, while the not yet amalgamated Midland Railway is advertised on the right. *Architect:* H. Branch

Bottom: The Longstaff newsroom (now reference library) at West Hill, Wandsworth. The photograph is of about 1905. Dr. G. D. Longstaff was the first Chairman of the Wandsworth Committee and his portrait hangs directly beneath the clock. Children were clearly allowed to use the room, which is lit by gas

Lecture Halls

In the days before radio and television, the illustrated lantern lecture reigned supreme. Large audiences could be guaranteed for well-known personalities, talking on subjects as diverse as the art treasures of Florence or intrepid adventures in darkest Patagonia.

Lecture halls were not numerous in early London public libraries, but where they were provided, the hard bentwood chairs and general no-nonsense decoration were proof of a formidable dedication to learning.

The lantern was an extremely temperamental piece of equipment and had to be coaxed into giving a good performance by a highly skilled operator. The outstanding problem was the amount of heat generated and it was advisable for those of easily offended susceptibilities, to remain at some distance from the operator, who on the not infrequent occasions when he touched the outside casing by mistake, was wont to relieve his feelings in colourful and forceful language.

Above: Not an illustration for a paperback version of the *Day of the Triffids*, but the Stoke Newington Central Library Lecture Hall prepared for some gentle palm court musical entertainment. An undated photograph, but probably Edwardian

Below: The Walthamstow Central Library Lecture Hall about 1909, when it was first opened. A very pleasant room with interesting decorations and fittings

Above right: The Croydon Public Libraries programme of talks, readings and exhibitions for October to December, 1910

Below right: This poster advertising a free lecture at Poplar on a stirring and patriotic theme is appropriately decorated with maple leaves

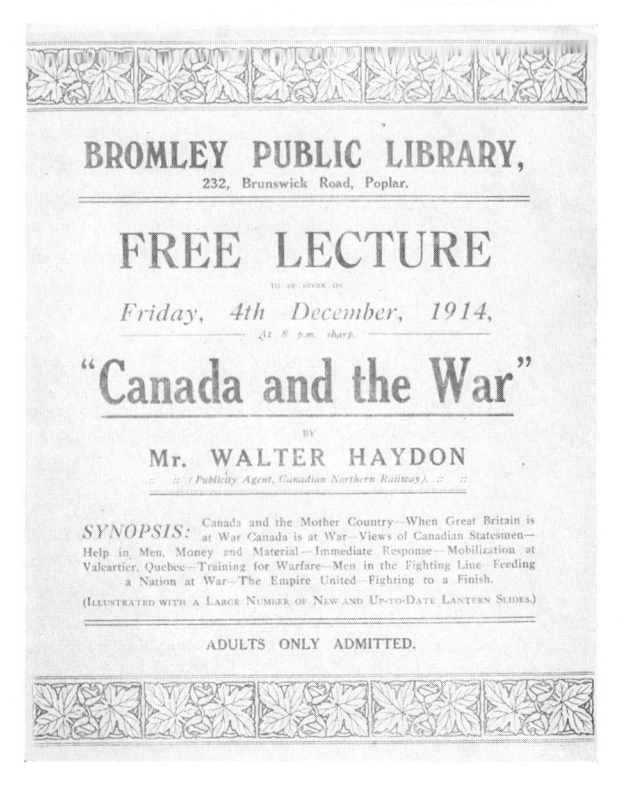

Cataloguing Departments, Catalogues and Classification Schemes

A cataloguing department was like a ship's engine room. Whatever radical changes of book selection policy might take place on the bridge, the staff of the department had to transform the chaos of newly arrived parcels into an orderly sequence of volumes on the shelves.

The nautical analogy is not altogether fanciful, as the department was frequently located in a basement or odd corner of a building, even though in theory there should have been good natural lighting.

It was also inevitable that the work room for repairing books, sticking in date labels, sending overdue notices and carrying out a hundred and one other odd jobs, should be next to the cataloguing department or even form a section of it.

In really badly designed buildings, this combined area also served as a staff room, so that a bubbling glue pot was near personal lockers and a gas stove rubbed uneasy shoulders with shelves carrying bibliographies and that no-hope collection of books, which had been removed from the public gaze, but never quite made the stack. Lucky indeed was the staff, whose needs had been considered carefully by the provision of a decently appointed room, where they could find some proper relaxation during a long working day.

The battle between open access and indicators was closely paralleled by that between classified and dictionary catalogues. Each type had its dedicated protagonists, who held passionately to their own preference, and had no time for those of the contrary view. To complicate matters, each type could naturally be produced on cards, slips or in printed form. In the early days of a library, when a bookstock was still relatively small, printing was obviously a great improvement on the handwritten cards or slips, which were general in the days before typewriters became common.

Sometimes an incoming Chief would change the type or form of catalogue and start a new sequence. The old catalogue would then naturally have no additions, but often more seriously, no withdrawals either. Older staff became highly skilful at threading their way through the resulting complexities and could judge to a nicety, whether an entry from a long abandoned catalogue actually represented a book in the basement store.

Two classification schemes held sway in the majority of London public libraries before the first world war. These were the decimal system of Melvil Dewey in all its various editions and the so-called classification of that great library developer and innovator, J. D. Brown. The latter flourished more in Greater London than the rest of the country and although surviving to a third edition, produced in 1939 by J. D. Stewart, has now disappeared entirely from the public library scene.

Chiefs tended to be great meddlers with classification schemes and delighted in producing half-baked variations for subjects dear to their hearts. Directly these enthusiasts were removed from the scene by promotion or retirement, the staff would hastily revert to standard practice and seal off the disaster area like an abandoned mine shaft. If they were unlucky, the incoming incumbent would repeat the process, until not one, but a whole series of dangerous workings had been created. The recognition and avoidance of these hazards meant that the uninitiated needed special training by those who had grown up in the system.

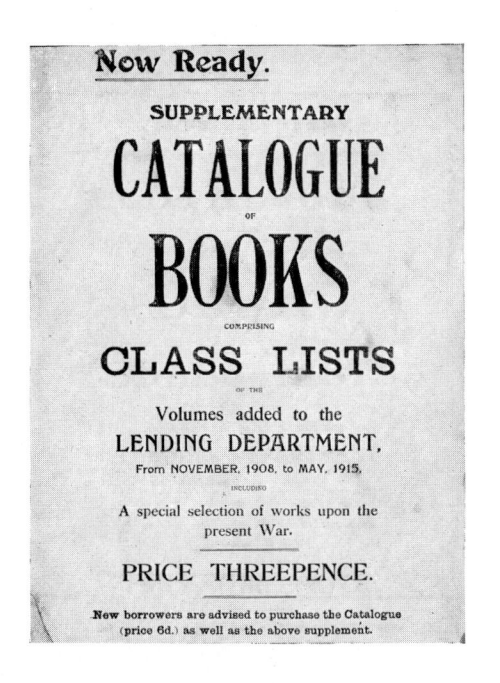

Left and right: Notices from Richmond of printed catalogues for sale

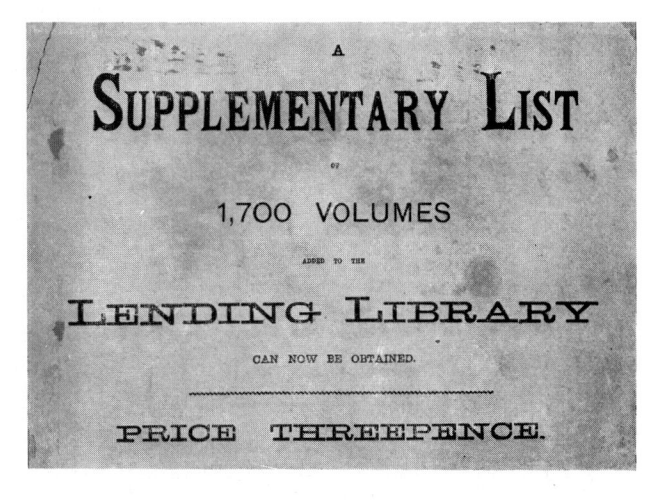

Above: The title page of the first public library catalogue in London

Above right: What was expected of every assistant. An example sheet from Libraco

Right: J. D. Stewart was Chief of Bermondsey from 1927 to 1950. When he was an assistant at Croydon in 1906, he applied for a post at Islington and was the successful candidate. As proof of his cataloguing ability, he sent a wide selection of handwritten cards with his application. They were obviously modelled on the 'disjoined hand' of the Libraco example sheet

Below: The seat on which you sat when working in a cataloguing department

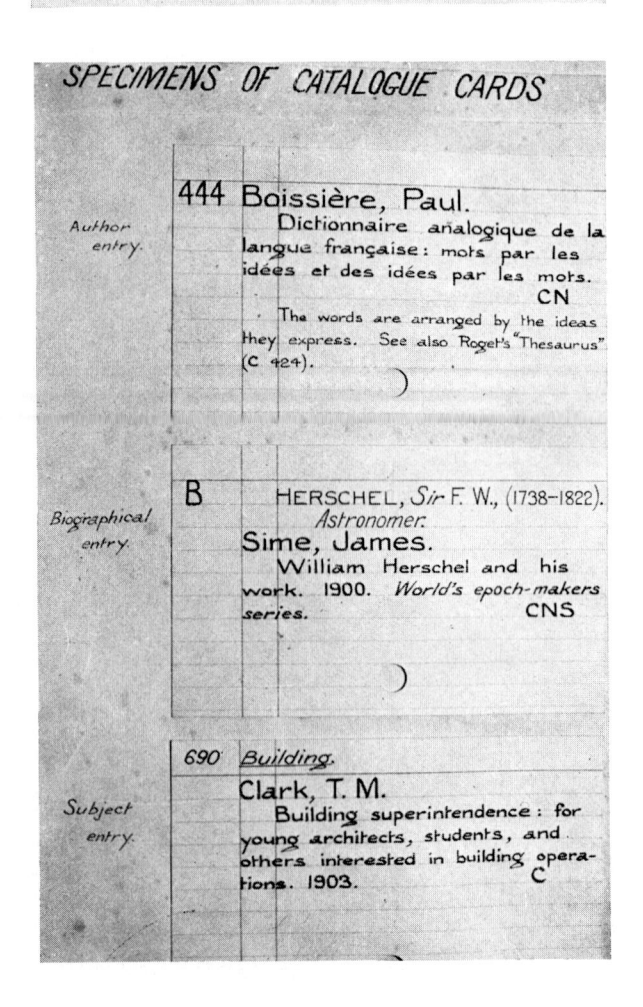

Above: This venerable card catalogue in the Guildhall Library was photographed in March 1895. It is pleasant to record that, although no longer in the public gaze, it is cherished and used by the staff behind the scenes

Books and Readers

It must be recorded, that while buildings, furniture and fittings loomed large in the minds of those setting up the first public libraries, books came a long way down the scale of priorities. This was inevitable, given the crippling burden of the penny rate limitation, which lasted until 1919. While a certain number of donations could be a valuable form of pump-priming, a too close reliance on this form of acquisition, meant a rapid descent into tattiness, with shelf-weary books forming a shabby collection of irregulars, instead of an army with pride and fire in its belly.

Even if the Victorians and Edwardians had ever heard of built-in obsolescence, they would have regarded the concept with contempt and shops advertised their wares with such phrases as 'no common rubbish' or 'will last a lifetime'. This was naturally true of binding and a row of books on a shelf represented a craftsman's art, lavished with care and skill.

Whether the skins that covered the books had come originally from goats or pigs, they were known to the irreverent as 'elephant's arse', and had all the durability of that long-lived pachyderm. No frivolity was allowed to creep in when it came to colour, as the decencies had to be observed. Among books on a shelf, sombre liturgical blacks alternated with deep ox-blood maroons, while conifer-forest greens rubbed shoulders with chocolate browns (plain, not milk). Blue was also allowed, but only if it resembled black so closely, that the two colours were virtually indistinguishable.

While binding of this standard could be expected to last a lifetime, mere paper and print gave up the ghost in far shorter order. If any assessment of the value of a bookstock had to be made, it was wise to open a large number of volumes, as splendid exteriors often hid interiors of the most unprepossessing kind.

Left: Mark Twain, the American writer, applies for a reader's ticket at Chelsea under his own name, S. L. Clemens. At the time he was a bankrupt and on a European lecture tour to revive his fortunes. The strain he was under shows in the way his signature and address fall off markedly to the right

Right: Alexander Glenny was the eighteen-year-old son of Captain Samuel Glenny of Great Field Farm. The latter commanded the guard of honour formed by D Company, 1st Volunteer Battalion, the Essex Regiment, at the opening ceremony of the first Barking Library on May 31st, 1889. He played a prominent part in the life of the community and was described as 'a man of commanding presence and very substantial proportions'. It is something of a miracle that this ticket should have survived at all. The present Barking Central Library was opened on June 10th, 1974 as a replacement for the previous one, which had been totally reconstructed internally, only to be destroyed by arson on April 4th, 1967. This ticket and its elaborate surround was literally pulled out from under a fireman's boot at the time of the fire and both bear marks of singeing

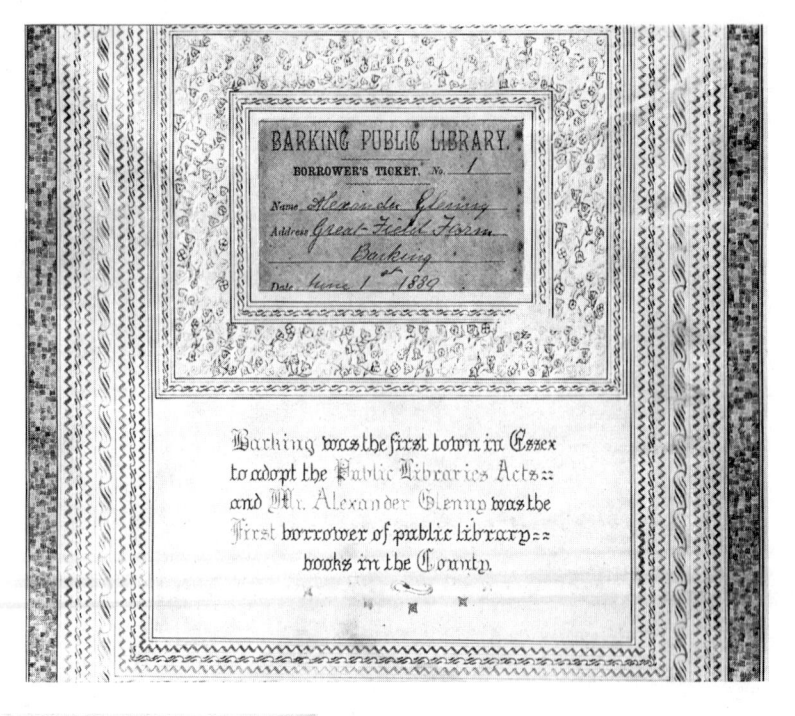

Left: John Passmore Edwards fills in a form to borrow Robinson's *History of Tottenham*. As this form is one of a batch coded 1/96 and Passmore Edwards attended the opening ceremony of Tottenham Central Library on February 12th, 1896, the later dating seems certain. It would be intriguing to know whether he was actually allowed to take it away from the building

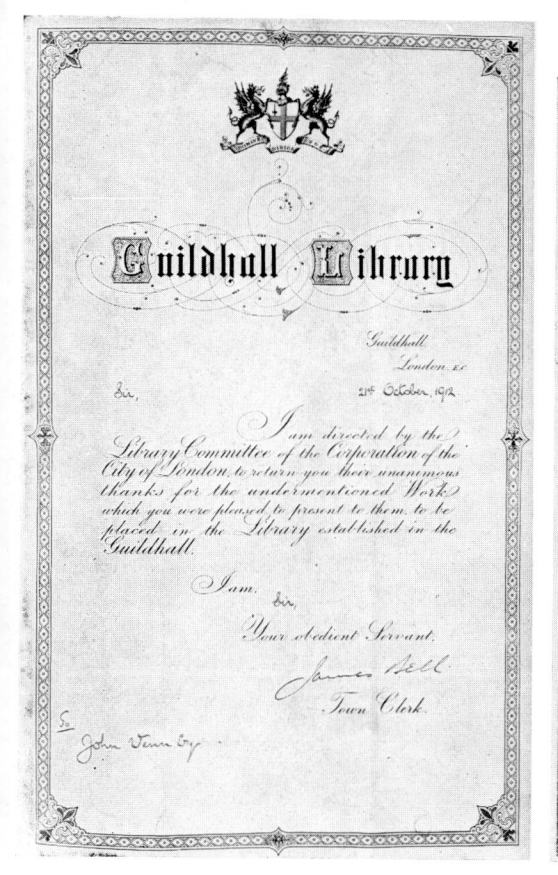

Above left: Not so much an acknowledgement, more an illuminated address. This fulsome document, of which the illustration is merely the front page, had room inside for donations to be listed and was roughly the size of a page of this book

Above centre: The controversy surrounding censorship in public libraries has a timeless quality. This leader writer in the *Westminster & Pimlico News* of September 6th, 1907, takes the City Council gently apart for excluding not sex but socialism

Above right: Alfred Cotgreave in a smart coat holding one of his more ingenious library devices at the high port. This is obviously intended to remove books from high shelves and presumably replace them again. The photograph is before 1885 when he was still Chief of Richmond. It is rather like a combination of a toasting fork and one of those scissor-operated pair of claws for putting pieces of coal on a fire. Did the idea come to him while toasting crumpets at home for tea one bleak Victorian winter Sunday evening and is one forgotten specimen still lurking in a corner of some library basement?

Below: Readers' suggestion books are always liable to contain amusing, if not downright abusive, observations. The one dated October 14th, 1895, is scathing about the lack of anything by Wagner, but there has been added the (staff?) comment 'not at present – too expensive'. The entries are from the suggestion book kept in the 1890's at the Victoria Branch of the Westminster Public Libraries

Chiefs

Although to mere junior assistants, he seemed second only to the Deity, a London chief librarian was often young when first appointed, badly paid and a not particularly important official of a parish or borough. There were tales of some men, who dressed like stockbrokers and were handed a fresh pair of white gloves every morning by the caretaker, so that they could test the amount of dust on the shelves; but they were few in number compared with those librarians, who had a really dedicated approach to the job.

For almost a century from the first Library Act of 1850 until the end of the second world war, it was rare to find graduates employed in the public library service and Greater London was no exception. Bad salaries and long hours meant that most Chiefs had received a Board School education, but this lack of formal training was offset by a devotion to their work.

Very little research has been done on the effect in this country of the wide selection of books made available by the public library service. It must, however, have contributed significantly to an informed public opinion over a great range of subjects and for this Chiefs and their staff can take a great deal of credit. The staying power of some men was truly phenomenal and the literary output of names like James Duff Brown and Berwick Sayers was such that it almost constituted a second occupation.

Not unnaturally Greater London was a mecca for provincial librarians and many well-known names in the profession spent their most productive years in the Capital. The Library Assistants' Association, which changed its name to the present Association of Assistant Librarians in 1922, was overwhelmingly a London based organisation until after the first world war and produced a steady stream of fiery young men, who naturally in the fullness of time became staid and respectable Chiefs.

Above: Two important London Chiefs of the period before the first world war. On the left is the romantic theosophist, L. Stanley Jast, who was Librarian of Croydon from 1898 to 1915

The photograph is of 1913. On the right is an 1899 photograph of James Duff Brown in his Clerkenwell days

Above: Henry William Bull was not a famous Chief, but held a long tenure of office at Wimbledon from 1896 to 1935. Here in a photograph of 1903, he looks relaxed and confident in the reference library

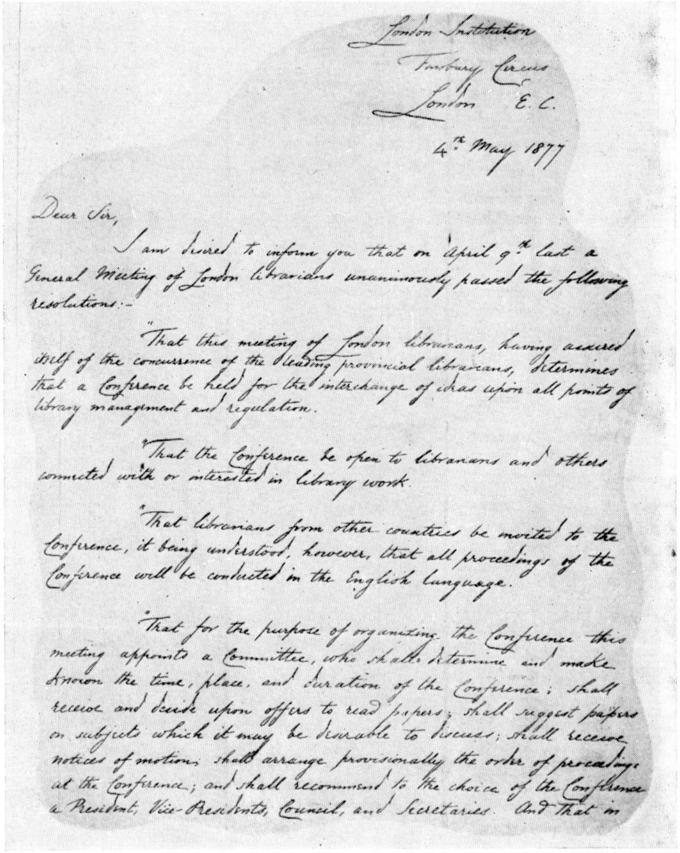

Above right: The first page of an historic letter. It was sent by Edward B. Nicholson, Librarian of the London Institution to a large number of librarians. It suggests the setting up of the 1877 conference, which led to the formation of the Library Association. It is clear that librarians in London played the leading initial role in the formation of the national professional body, through the meeting convened on April 9th, 1877

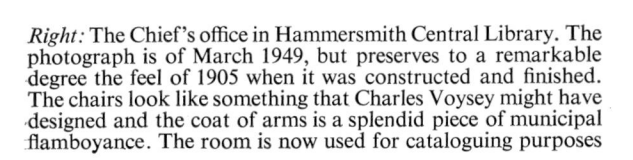

Right: The Chief's office in Hammersmith Central Library. The photograph is of March 1949, but preserves to a remarkable degree the feel of 1905 when it was constructed and finished. The chairs look like something that Charles Voysey might have designed and the coat of arms is a splendid piece of municipal flamboyance. The room is now used for cataloguing purposes

Above: The Librarian's office at the Guildhall, in use from 1872 to 1974. A sketch by Dennis Flanders produced in the 1970's, but showing the room with its original fitments from the 1870's. The Guildhall Library was moved to a new building in 1974 and the old building is to be used for other Corporation purposes

Left: Enfield Central Library in Cecil Road. A photograph showing the Chief's office in 1912. The inkwell, sit-up-and-beg typewriter and roll-top desk are all worthy of note

Library Staff

If conditions for Chiefs were not good, the life of the rest of the staff was even worse. Long hours, split duties and drab work rooms added up to a somewhat monotonous existence. In addition, studying for professional examinations had to be undertaken in whatever spare time remained.

Although the exceptionally able managed to rise above these impediments, there was clearly less movement from authority to authority to gain promotion and more people than today passed all their working life in one area. It should perhaps be emphasised that conditions generally in libraries were no better or worse, than those in a wide range of professional and clerical jobs in the period under consideration.

One aspect of the whole matter about which, for obvious reasons, there is very little information, was the practice of moonlighting or taking second jobs. This is especially true if library premises were being used by those showing more initiative than discretion, although a Nelsonian blind eye on the part of those in authority was obviously a necessary concomitant to the success of any of these unofficial business ventures.

The range and variety of these enterprises can only be described as astonishing. There were the mundane, such as working an insurance or encyclopaedia sales round; the highly entrepreneurial, exemplified by a makeshift hairdressing salon in an unused room at the rear of a branch library; and the frankly incredible, best represented by the growing of mushrooms on spoil heaps, left after the construction of foundations at another branch library.

Out of hours, there were bicycle trips to Hatfield House and jaunts down the Thames arranged by staff associations, or totally informally, as the spirit moved. After picnics followed by liquid refreshment in pubs or temperance hotels, according to inclination, groups were sometimes persuaded to pose; and looking at such photographs, it is painful to recall how so much gaiety and enjoyment was to be swept away by the holocaust of the first world war.

Above: A sketch of librarians on the Guildhall staff dated October 14th, 1885. It was made by Austin Travers Young, a nephew of Bernard Kettle. From left to right the four people are J. E. Thompson, C. Welch, B. Kettle and W. H. Overall. The Guildhall Librarian at the time was Overall and Bernard Kettle was to assume this office in 1909

Right: High jinks for the Lambeth staff on their annual beano on the South Coast. Brighton and Eastbourne were favoured venues, as they were easy of access by rail from Lambeth. An elaborate programme was printed with all sorts of literary quips and quotations and this typical cover is from the one produced in 1899

Below: No nonsense about graduates

AN ASSISTANT WANTED.

AGE ABOUT 15.

LAMBETH LIBRARIES.

Annual Excursion.

FRIDAY, JULY 28th, 1899,

TO

BRIGHTON.

"Variety's the very spice of life
That gives it all its flavor." —*Cowper*

Above: As in many other ways, J. D. Brown was a pioneer in the employment of women on his staff. In this undated photograph, taken during his tenure of office at Islington from 1905 to 1914, he is seen surrounded by a bevy of female talent. It is a pity that the soft focus of the photograph does not do them full justice

Right: The Croydon staff. A photograph taken almost certainly in 1895. Thomas Johnston, the then Chief sits in the middle of the centre row and a youthful E. A. Savage stands second from the left in the back row

Below: A meeting of the Library Assistants' Association photographed in the Edwardian period in the grounds of West Hill Library, Wandsworth. Is Berwick Sayers the fourth person from the left in the front standing row? If so, this dates the picture definitely beyond 1904, when Sayers moved to Croydon. Whatever the date, the assembled throng seems extremely well dressed and full of the joys of the occasion

Above: E. E. Larner. A long-distance walker, who was a member of the Hammersmith staff. He represented Britain in the 1908 Olympics and came fifth in the ten mile walk. This photograph was taken at Epsom about 1903 and shows him striding out ahead at the beginning of a long distance event

Above: W. B. Macdouall, Branch Librarian at Shepherd's Bush, Hammersmith, gave the Albion Brewery some competition by growing a vine up the side of the building and harvesting the Black Hambro grapes seen at the top of the page. The photograph of the grapes is dated 1911 and so presumably is this one of wives and children of staff taking their ease under the awning. The railway viaduct is part of a section just south of Shepherd's Bush Station on the then Metropolitan Railway (now the Metropolitan Line of London Transport)

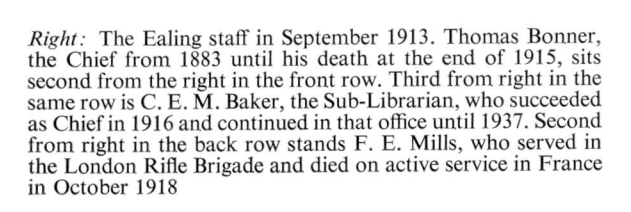

Right: The Ealing staff in September 1913. Thomas Bonner, the Chief from 1883 until his death at the end of 1915, sits second from the right in the front row. Third from right in the same row is C. E. M. Baker, the Sub-Librarian, who succeeded as Chief in 1916 and continued in that office until 1937. Second from right in the back row stands F. E. Mills, who served in the London Rifle Brigade and died on active service in France in October 1918

Caretakers and Cleaners

The caretaker was a formidable personage in his own right and one of the key figures in the organisation of any library. Chief librarians were wont to regard him as a personal servant but he retained his own independence to a considerable degree. He was often a former sergeant-major or chief petty officer and could be counted on to maintain a ferociously martial appearance, especially with local layabouts and tramps, who tried to make the newsroom their permanent abode.

His official duties were legion, the most important being to stoke a large coke boiler in the basement at regular intervals, rather as one would feed a tutelary deity in more primitive societies. His personal cubby hole was a fiercely guarded kingdom into which he would retreat for large mugs of tea, a quiet fag and the sporting pages of the more popular newspapers.

Unofficial duties included an early warning system for the staff at the approach of the Chief, which was far more effective than radar, the carrying of betting slips and the purchase of cigarettes as necessary. From time to time he could be prevailed upon to cover a stone floor with water and mop it up again, on the good Services' principle, that what is wet is clean. However, the main cleaning he left to women specially engaged for the purpose and they maintained a motherly eye on the general welfare of the younger staff.

It happened occasionally, that a newly-appointed Chief would rashly seek to curtail some of the privileges, which the caretaker had enjoyed over many years. This move was usually countered by a campaign of dumb insolence and calculated disobedience, which nevertheless managed to remain on the right side of the law by a hairsbreadth. The situation resolved itself only when both sides felt that enough face had been restored in best approved Chinese manner. When this happened, the whole staff breathed a sigh of relief.

Left: Wimbledon Library in 1903. The Caretaker is F. Gare. He is reported as having been a great character

Right: Advertisement for a porter, cleaner and messenger at Bow Library. Presumably this means an annual increment of 10/-, so that the maximum salary would be reached at the end of thirteen years' service

Below: Early vacuum cleaners. The 'Harvey' was designed to cover large areas and the 'Universal' for smaller jobs

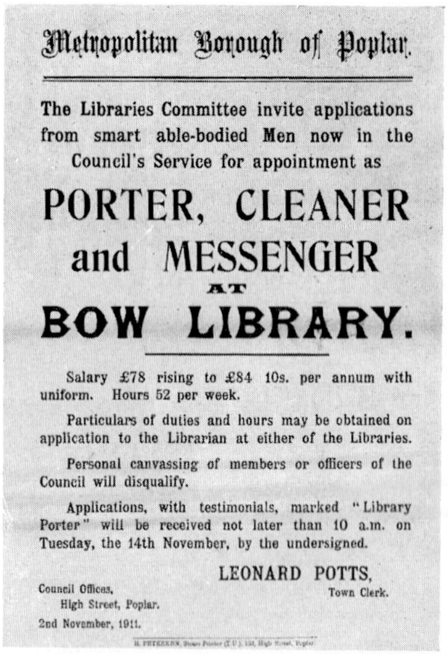

Metropolitan Borough of Poplar.

The Libraries Committee invite applications from smart able-bodied Men now in the Council's Service for appointment as

PORTER, CLEANER and MESSENGER AT BOW LIBRARY.

Salary £78 rising to £84 10s. per annum with uniform. Hours 52 per week.

Particulars of duties and hours may be obtained on application to the Librarian at either of the Libraries.

Personal canvassing of members or officers of the Council will disqualify.

Applications, with testimonials, marked "Library Porter" will be received not later than 10 a.m. on Tuesday, the 14th November, by the undersigned.

LEONARD POTTS,
Council Offices, Town Clerk.
High Street, Poplar.
2nd November, 1911.

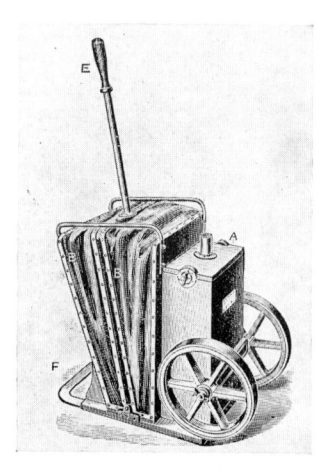

Above: Stephen Butt, 1st class attendant at the Guildhall Library. An undated photograph about which there are no further details

Below: With feather dusters at the ready. Two cleaners at West Ham Central Library in 1898, presumably about the time of the opening of the building

Above: Monarch of all he surveys. The Caretaker at Putney Library in the 1890's
Below: The same scene as on the left, but now under the eagle eye of the Head Caretaker. The lady cleaner has been so overcome by the occasion, that she has put on a flowered bonnet. This is presumably a slightly later photograph, as the entrance has now been festooned with prohibitory notices. The one on the extreme right is headed ominously 'Spitting'

Committees and Finance

As far as local councillors were concerned, public libraries could hardly have been termed big business. Any incipient recklessness with the ratepayers' money was instantly curbed by the straitjacket of the penny rate limitations. However, members of libraries committees hardly ever showed inclinations of this kind. On the contrary they were likely to be sober citizens, who watched the pennies carefully. Either they were young councillors learning the ropes on a committee, where it was felt they could do no harm, or elderly aldermen put out to grass for having fallen foul of the leading lights in their own political grouping. Occasionally a former university don or retired schoolmaster was co-opted, in order to give a faint air of scholarship to an otherwise somewhat low-brow assemblage.

In these enlightened days when most Chiefs are so enmeshed in the toils of corporate management that they can hardly distinguish a novel from a two pound bag of sugar at ten paces, it may come as something of a surprise to younger librarians, that one of the prime functions of a committee was to choose books. This was done with great deliberation and it was Darwin and his views on monkeys, rather than *Linda Lovelace* or *Last Exit to Brooklyn*, that gave cause for concern. Naturally, when a committee had examined books, it then borrowed them to read before this privilege was extended to the general public.

The art of handling a committee was, and still remains, a fascinating subject in its own right. It was not always the great names in librarianship that succeeded the best, but often somebody long since forgotten, who nevertheless had the happy knack of putting people at ease and lightening the atmosphere with an appropriate joke or apposite remark, if the going started to be rough. Above all, a committee hated being patronised and this was often the downfall of the insensitive or unwary.

Although the main financial support for libraries came from the rates, other methods for raising a little supplementary income were not unknown. Apart from the common one of charging fines for overdue books, two of the more unlikely were a church-style offertory box in one authority and a bequest form at the end of another authority's annual report. It is an ironic thought, that both of these latter may well be in fashion again during the next decade.

Above: The combined committee room and office for the Librarian at Putney about 1910. The fittings and furniture were of a high standard because of its function. The panelling and the light fitment are especially noteworthy

Above: The Public Library Committee of Brentford for the municipal year 1900/1901. Fred Turner, the Librarian, stands slightly to the left of the door and seems undernourished compared with the ample committee members, by whom he is surrounded. His enormous black moustache is a particularly fine specimen of its kind

Below left: The list of duties of the Libraries Sub-Committee at Wandsworth in 1905. The Libraries Committee itself seems to have been totally superfluous except to act as a large rubber stamp

Below right: A letter of appointment for a Wandsworth Library Commissioner soon after the adoption of the Acts

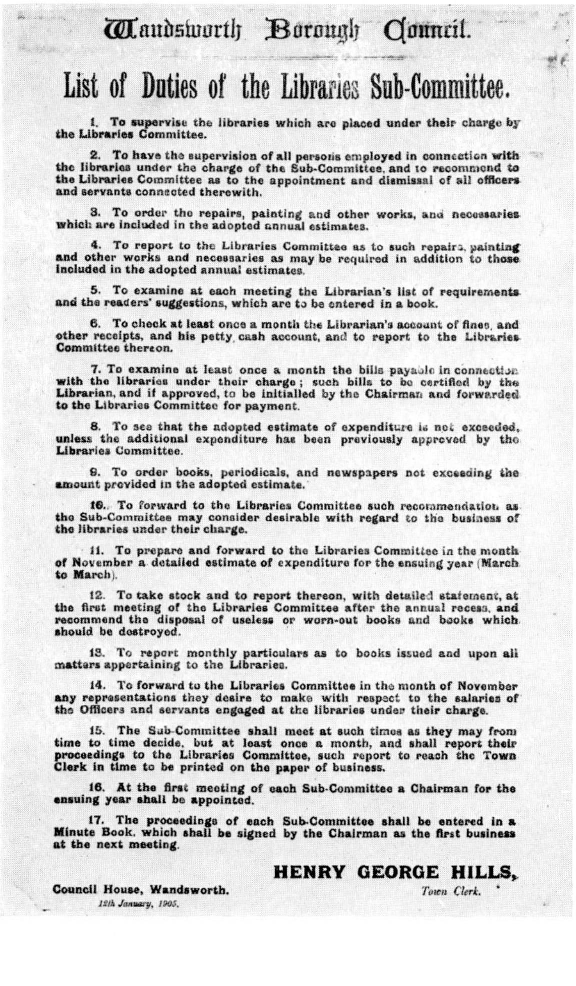

Wandsworth Borough Council.

List of Duties of the Libraries Sub-Committee.

1. To supervise the libraries which are placed under their charge by the Libraries Committee.

2. To have the supervision of all persons employed in connection with the libraries under the charge of the Sub-Committee, and to recommend to the Libraries Committee as to the appointment and dismissal of all officers and servants connected therewith.

3. To order the repairs, painting and other works, and necessaries which are included in the adopted annual estimates.

4. To report to the Libraries Committee as to such repairs, painting and other works and necessaries as may be required in addition to those included in the adopted annual estimates.

5. To examine at each meeting the Librarian's list of requirements and the readers' suggestions, which are to be entered in a book.

6. To check at least once a month the Librarian's account of fines, and other receipts, and his petty cash account, and to report to the Libraries Committee thereon.

7. To examine at least once a month the bills payable in connection with the libraries under their charge; such bills to be certified by the Librarian, and if approved, to be initialled by the Chairman and forwarded to the Libraries Committee for payment.

8. To see that the adopted estimate of expenditure is not exceeded, unless the additional expenditure has been previously approved by the Libraries Committee.

9. To order books, periodicals, and newspapers not exceeding the amount provided in the adopted estimate.

10. To forward to the Libraries Committee such recommendation as the Sub-Committee may consider desirable with regard to the business of the libraries under their charge.

11. To prepare and forward to the Libraries Committee in the month of November a detailed estimate of expenditure for the ensuing year (March to March).

12. To take stock and to report thereon, with detailed statement, at the first meeting of the Libraries Committee after the annual recess, and recommend the disposal of useless or worn-out books and books which should be destroyed.

13. To report monthly particulars as to books issued and upon all matters appertaining to the Libraries.

14. To forward to the Libraries Committee in the month of November any representations they desire to make with respect to the salaries of the Officers and servants engaged at the libraries under their charge.

15. The Sub-Committee shall meet at such times as they may from time to time decide, but at least once a month, and shall report their proceedings to the Libraries Committee, such report to reach the Town Clerk in time to be printed on the paper of business.

16. At the first meeting of each Sub-Committee a Chairman for the ensuing year shall be appointed.

17. The proceedings of each Sub-Committee shall be entered in a Minute Book, which shall be signed by the Chairman as the first business at the next meeting.

HENRY GEORGE HILLS,
Council House, Wandsworth.   Town Clerk.
12th January, 1905.

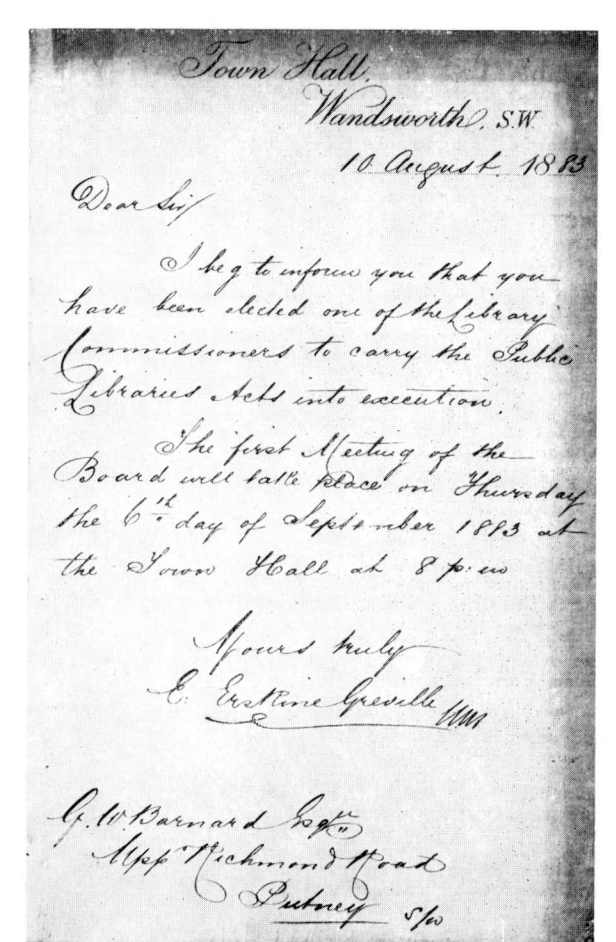

Town Hall,
Wandsworth, S.W.
10 August 1883

Dear Sir,

I beg to inform you that you have been elected one of the Library Commissioners to carry the Public Libraries Acts into execution.

The first Meeting of the Board will take place on Thursday the 6th day of September 1883 at the Town Hall at 8 p.m.

Yours truly
E. Erskine Greville

G. W. Barnard Esq.
Mps Richmond Road
Putney

The Vestry of the Parish of

BROMLEY SAINT LEONARD.

Public Libraries & Museums.

SOUTH BROMLEY BRANCH:
126, BRUNSWICK ROAD, E.

RULES AND REGULATIONS.

AUGUST, 1896.

PRINTED BY F. HASTIE, (SOCIETY HOUSE) 11, DEWBERRY STREET, E.
1896.

BOROUGH OF KINGSTON-UPON-THAMES.

PUBLIC LIBRARY.

RULES & REGULATIONS.

GENERAL.

1.—The Librarian shall have the general charge of the Library, and shall be responsible for the safe keeping of the books, and all other property.

2.—Intoxicated, disorderly, or otherwise offensive persons shall not be allowed in the Library, nor shall dogs or other animals be admitted. Talking, smoking, spitting, and partaking of refreshments in the Library shall not be permitted.

3.—It is expressly forbidden to take away any book, map, newspaper, magazine, or other article of Library property, except books lent from the Lending Department, or to cut, mark, tear, or otherwise deface or destroy the same. Any person so offending shall be liable to a prosecution under the Statute 24 and 25 Victoria, cap. 97. Such papers, books, &c., as are accessible to the public must be returned to their proper table or rack when done with. The papers on the stands must not be moved.

4.—No directory, newspaper, periodical, or magazine shall be retained longer than ten minutes after it has been asked for by another reader.

Above: One of the duties of a Committee was to make rules and regulations. On the left is the front page of such a document at Bromley St. Leonard, Poplar, in August 1896 and on the right the first four rules and regulations passed at Kingston upon Thames a year earlier

Right and below right: Many other methods in addition to raising a rate were tried in order to produce income for library services. These ranged from the offertory box and bequest form approach on the right, through collecting cards at the bottom right, to the concerts and special theatrical performances detailed on the next page

Below left: The cost of running a library service in the Edwardian period. An abstract of accounts from Islington

---

THIS Box has been placed here for the convenience of Visitors who wish to contribute towards the support of the Library.

Loan Repayments.—3½ per cent.

	1906-7	1907-8	1908-9	1909-10	1910-11	1911-12	1912-13
	£	£	£	£	£	£	£
North	164	161	157	153	149	145	141
West	164	161	157	153	149	145	141
Central	...	123	121	119	117	115	113
East	...	...	164	161	157	153	149
South	...	...	...	164	161	157	153
	£328	£445	£599	£750	£733	£715	£697

Amount of Loans for excess on Buildings over Carnegie gift:—

North	£2,400
West	2,400
Central	1,800
East	2,400
South	2,400
	£11,400 in round figures.

Estimated Expenditure, 1906-7 to 1912-13.

Income

	1906-7	1907-8	1908-9	1909-10	1910-11	1911-12	1912-13
	£	£	£	£	£	£	£
Library Rate	7,700	7,700	7,700	7,700	7,700	7,700	7,700
Cash Receipts	100	240	320	400	400	400	400
Balance, 1905-6	6,500	1,350	899	106	251	323	303
	£14,300	£9,290	£8,919	£8,206	£8,351	£8,423	£8,403

Expenditure.

	1906-7	1907-8	1908-9	1909-10	1910-11	1911-12	1912-13
Lighting	165	446	566	731	731	731	731
Heating	25	50	65	85	85	85	85
Water	18	23	30	45	45	45	45
Fittings and Repairs	55	130	160	190	190	190	190
Cleaning	20	55	70	85	85	85	85
Telephones	7	21	28	35	35	35	35
Insurance	...	35	42	50	50	50	50
Rent	13	...	...	...	...	...	...
Rates	55	...	...	...	...	...	...
	16	30	40	50	50	50	50
Periodicals	136	280	360	440	440	440	440
Binding	50	100	260	320	320	320	320
Salaries	1,500	1,700	2,500	2,800	2,900	3,000	3,265
Stationery	60	40	50	60	60	60	60
Printing	150	100	110	130	120	130	130
Postages	10	20	25	30	30	30	30
Contingences	200	200	100	400	400	400	400
Fittings, furniture	5,719	1,300	1,300	—	—	—	—
Sites Loans	423	416	508	554	554	554	554
Building Loans	328	445	599	750	733	715	697
TOTALS	8,950	5,391	6,813	6,755	6,828	6,920	7,167
Books	4,000	3,000	2,000	1,200	1,200	1,200	1,200
Balance	1,350	899	106	251	323	303	36
	£14,300	£9,290	£8,919	£8,206	£8,351	£8,423	£8,403

FORM OF BEQUEST.

I bequeath out of such part of my personal estate as may by Law be bequeathed for such purposes, to the Free Library Committee of the Brentford Public Library, in the County of Middlesex, the sum of .... free from Legacy Duty, for the benefit of the Public Library of the said town, to be expended in such a way as they may deem expedient; and I direct that the receipt of the Chairman for the time being be an efficient discharge for the same legacy.

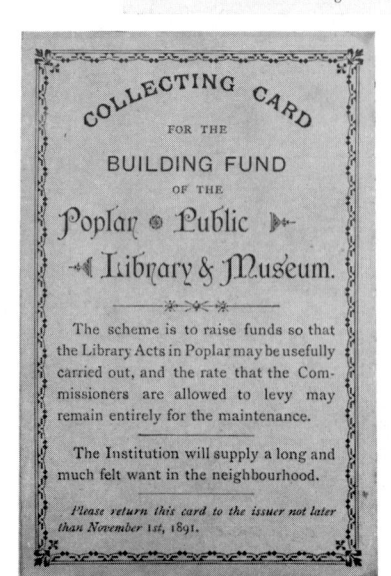

COLLECTING CARD

FOR THE

BUILDING FUND

OF THE

Poplar Public Library & Museum.

The scheme is to raise funds so that the Library Acts in Poplar may be usefully carried out, and the rate that the Commissioners are allowed to levy may remain entirely for the maintenance.

The Institution will supply a long and much felt want in the neighbourhood.

Please return this card to the issuer not later than November 1st, 1891.

Ealing Free Library.

The Bearer of this Card, Mr. ....

is authorised by the Free Library Committee to collect on behalf of the Workmen's Free Library Fund.

(*Signed*)

THOMAS BONNER,
Secretary and Librarian.

R. GAMBLE,
Secretary to the Fund.

LYRIC HALL, EALING

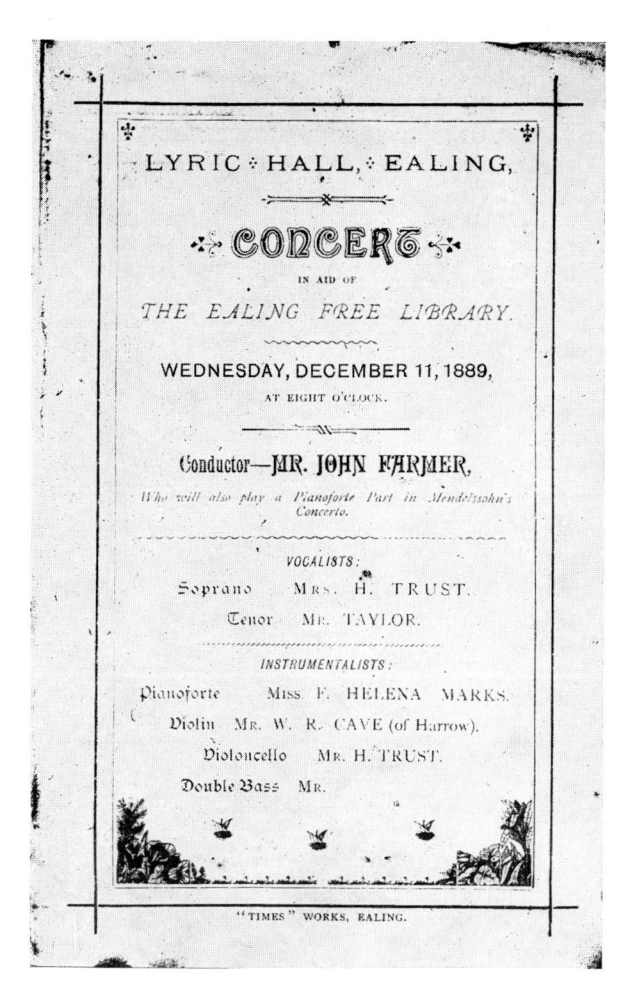

CONCERT
IN AID OF
THE EALING FREE LIBRARY.

WEDNESDAY, DECEMBER 11, 1889,
AT EIGHT O'CLOCK.

Conductor—MR. JOHN FARMER,
Who will also play a Pianoforte Part in Mendelssohn's Concerto.

VOCALISTS:
Soprano — MRS. H. TRUST.
Tenor — MR. TAYLOR.

INSTRUMENTALISTS:
Pianoforte — Miss F. HELENA MARKS.
Violin — MR. W. R. CAVE (of Harrow).
Violoncello — MR. H. TRUST.
Double Bass — MR.

"TIMES" WORKS, EALING.

TOWN HALL, WANDSWORTH.

A GRAND EVENING CONCERT
WILL BE GIVEN BY
MISS LILIAN GREVILLE,
(OF THE ROYAL ACADEMY OF MUSIC).

ON TUESDAY, NOVEMBER 27TH, 1883,
IN AID OF THE BUILDING FUND OF THE
FREE LIBRARY FOR WANDSWORTH;

UNDER THE IMMEDIATE PATRONAGE OF:
SIR HENRY PEEK, BART., M.P. — LADY PEEK.
SIR TREVOR LAWRENCE, BART., M.P. — LADY LAWRENCE.
SIR THOMAS GABRIEL, BART. — LADY GABRIEL.
JOHN MORLEY, ESQ., M.P.
H. G. BAINBRIDGE, ESQ.,

Miss MEINERTZHAGEN, Wimbledon Park — Mrs. PFEIFFER, West Hill.
Mrs. CZARNIKOW, Elm Court, Mitcham — Mrs. DAVIS, Earlsfield, Wandsworth Common.
*Mrs. ELLIS, Gower House, Melrose Road, Southfields. — *Mrs. GREVILLE, Gerard Lodge, Southfields.
*Mrs. PAUL, High Street, Putney. — *Mrs. SINCLAIR, Woodville, Upper Richmond Road.
Mrs. HEWETSON, The Canons, Mitcham. — Mrs. GILBERT, The Chaplain's House, Wandsworth Common.
*Mrs. DEVEY, Lucan Lodge, Clapham Park.

The following Artistes have kindly consented to give their services:—
Vocalists—
MISS PATTI WINTER.
MISS CATHERINE TALBOT.
MISS LILIAN GREVILLE.
MR. DYVED LEWIS (THE WELSH TENOR).
MR. COPLAND.

Pianoforte, ... MISS MARGARET DEVEY, R.A.M.
Violin ... MR. FREDERICK HALL.
Recitations by ... MRS. JULIET ANDERSON.
Conductor ... MR. E. O. KIVER, R.A.M.
(*Professor Putney College of Music.*)

DOORS OPEN AT 7.30. / COMMENCE AT EIGHT O'CLOCK.
Stalls 5s. Reserved Seats 3s. Admission One Shilling.
Tickets may be obtained of the Lady Patronesses marked (*); at BURLEIGH'S Libraries, Wandsworth and Putney; Mr. BELL, Post Office, Wandsworth; Mr. PINK, Stationer, Gordon Terrace, Putney; at the Town Hall, Wandsworth; and at STONEHEWER'S Printing Works, High Street, Wandsworth.

STONEHEWER, Steam Printer, High Street, Wandsworth.

OLD RICHMOND THEATRE & EDMUND KEAN'S HOUSE, pulled down in 1884.

THE NEW THEATRE,
CASTLE ASSEMBLY ROOMS,
RICHMOND, SURREY.

PROPRIETOR — Mr. F. C. MOUFLET.

UNDER THE DIRECTION OF — Mr. HORACE LENNARD.

EASTER MONDAY, APRIL 7th, 1890.

SPECIAL MATINEE
FOR THE BENEFIT OF
The Richmond Free Public Library,
ON THE OCCASION OF
THE OPENING OF THE THEATRE.

PROGRAMME — THREEPENCE.

Prologue
Written by FREDERICK BINGHAM, ESQ.,
AND SPOKEN BY
MRS. LANGTRY,
At the Opening of the New Richmond Theatre,
EASTER MONDAY, 1890.

FRIENDS of the Drama, lovers of the Play
Assembled in this little house to-day,
To you our welcome and our thanks we give,
You, by whose favour long we hope to live;
You, who our venture with success can crown,
And give the Richmond Stage renewed renown.
The Richmond Stage! What recollections rise
As I those words pronounce. Before my eyes
I see the quaint old playhouse on the Green
Where Quin and Kemble, Cooke, "the wondrous [Kean,"
Macready—all who won Fame's greenest bays
Gave life to language in the olden days;
Where Siddons reigned in her majestic might!
Where Jordan's winsome laugh bade care grow [light;
Where Munden, Liston, Quick, and many more
Such merry fellows raised the frequent roar;
Where too the tyro—fearing—hoping—came
To take the weary road which led to fame;—
Charles Mathews, sword in hand, determin'd, bold
And Helen Faucit, heart with dread grown cold.
That little playhouse from our sight has gone,
It had outlived its day and night came on:

But now another morn is breaking here
Whilst all around is bright, serene and clear;
The Muses now no longer forced to roam
Again in Richmond find a worthy home.

Yonder at rest beneath an ancient tower
Sleeps Edmund Kean; who often spent an hour
At the old "Castle," which stood on this spot
And there, carousing, stage-fatigues forgot;
The ground is sacred to his memory fond,
And here, in hope that fortune will respond
To our appeal and help the Richmond Play
We open to the world our doors to-day.
Now royal Richmond's veterans and sons
In whom the love of things theatric runs,
And you, sweet lasses of her far-famed Hill,
Help us this old dramatic soil to till.
The stream which is your pride, in days of yore
Good fortune to the "Castle" often bore;
And may the kindly river of Success
Flow on to us in all unboundedness.
Down from its head the Thames will ever glide,
But from another *source* must flow the tide
Which bears prosperity within our view,
And, friends, that source we hope to find in *you*.

Above: Two concerts in aid of the public libraries in Ealing and Wandsworth and a special matinee for the benefit of Richmond Public Libraries. The Ealing programme unfortunately had to go to press before anybody could actually sign up a competent double bass and the main attraction at Richmond after Mrs. Langtry's prologue was a dramatised version of Bardell *v* Pickwick

Transport

Very little detail has survived about the transport of books between libraries in a borough. Because the service in Greater London had been set up in many instances by separate parishes and only later amalgamated, it seems not unreasonable to assume a high degree of self-sufficiency in bookstock.

East Ham, however, possessed a tricycle in the style of those used by the itinerant salesmen of Walls' sausages and ice-creams, while Croydon worked out an ingenious system using local trams. An assistant put a parcel of books on a tram, noted its number and the time and returned to his branch. He then telephoned the branch to which the parcel had been consigned, and asked somebody to make appropriate arrangements for its collection. Sadly, no photographs have survived.

The Shadow of War

Librarians in common with everybody else, were caught up in the maelstrom of the first world war and inevitably many never came back to resume their careers after 1918. Servicemen in uniform presented a brave appearance, but they were facing a world totally different from anything they had known before. Even after 1914, public librarianship in Greater London, as in the rest of the Country, was still in its pioneering days and developments after that date deserve their own story in pictorial form.

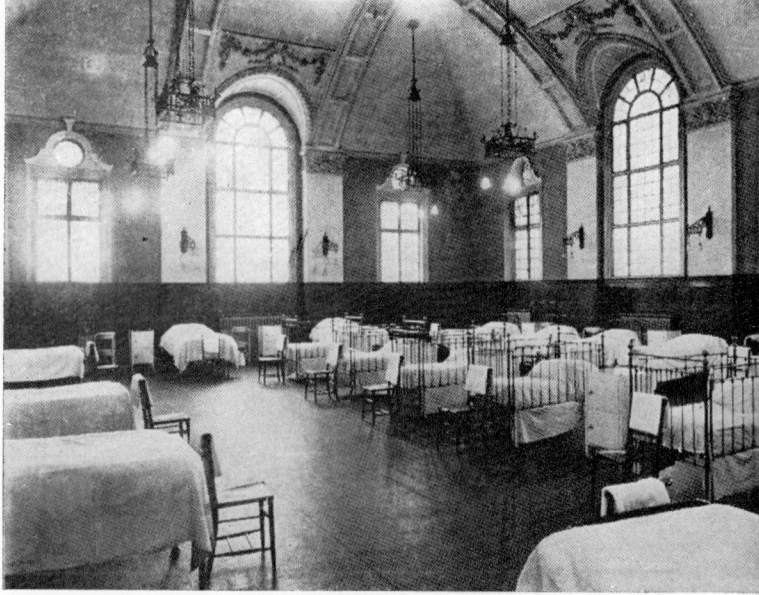

Above: On the left, Captain J. D. Stewart from the Islington staff. A 1915 photograph in uniform. He was a stalwart of the London and Home Counties Branch and the J. D. Stewart Bursary is named after him. On the right, Walthamstow Central Library prepared for use as a hospital, also of about 1915

Acknowledgements

It gives me particular pleasure as the Librarian of a London Borough to thank the Chief Librarians of the London Boroughs, the City of London and the City of Westminster, for permission to reproduce the photographs and other illustrations, which make up this work. Wherever I have gone, I have been met with the utmost kindness and refreshment upon the way.

A special word is also due to the Reference Librarians and Local History Librarians of London, who by their combined knowledge and wisdom, produced such a wealth of material for my inspection, that only a fraction of it could be included. It was a great personal delight to meet and talk to such charming people in their own libraries.

As in previous works, I am greatly indebted to my wife for her professional advice as an architectural historian and to Miss Margaret Marshall, the Reference Librarian of the Watford Branch of the Hertfordshire Library Service, for undertaking the tedious and difficult task of proof reading.

Suggestions for Further Reading

Thomas Kelly's specially commissioned *History of Public Libraries in Great Britain 1845–1965* (Library Association, 1973 – new edition in preparation) contains such an extensive bibliography, that it would be pointless to repeat its contents in a work of this kind. The reader seeking general background information about the public library movement before the first world war will find here the majority of what is required.

Firstly there are works written at the time and secondly critical and evaluative books of more recent date, which seek to give the subject perspective. Nor should professional library periodicals of the period be neglected, as they often have a freshness and immediacy lacking in the material written at greater leisure. Two more recent and extremely useful specialised bibliographies are entitled *British Library History* and are edited by Denis Keeling. Both are published by the Library Association; the first covering the years 1962–68 appeared in 1972 and the second, covering 1969–72, in 1975.

When this groundwork has been done, it is time to look more closely at the London scene. The best point of departure is the *Directory of London Public Libraries*, edited by K. R. McColvin (Association of London Chief Librarians). The fifth edition is the current one and there is a sixth in preparation. Not only does it list all library buildings under the names of the post-1965 London Boroughs, but also gives a great deal of information about the services provided. Earlier editions are already collectors' items, but the fourth edition of 1970 still lists the old authorities, that went to make up the new London Boroughs. It is especially helpful to those outside the Capital, as it also lists the village and district names, which I refer to in the General Introduction, and again gives the new London Borough equivalent.

At the same time it is as well to consult three works on London Local Government, Chapter VIII of K. B. Smellie's *A History of Local Government* (Allen & Unwin – 4th edition, 1968) deals with London from 1835 to 1967 as simply as a very complicated subject allows. This should be followed W. Eric Jackson's *Achievement: a short history of the L.C.C.* (Longmans, 1965) and *A Century of Municipal Progress 1835–1935* edited by Harold Laski (Allen & Unwin, 1935). Chapter XI is by L. Stanley Jast and deals with public libraries. It has a short but very good basic reading list, which can still be used with great profit. These should be followed by two unpublished works. The first is by P. M. Whiteman and is entitled *The Establishment of Public Libraries and the Unit of Local Government in London to 1900* (M.A. Thesis, Belfast, 1969). The second by D. Jones is called *The History of Rate-Supported Public Libraries in London: 1850–1900* (M.A. Thesis, London, 1972).

The next step is to approach the local history librarians and archivists of a particular area, in which you may be interested, and ask to see what source material about their own library systems is available. This consists of library committee minute books, newspaper cuttings, photographs, pamphlets, programmes for library stone-laying and opening ceremonies and perhaps a selection of past publicity material. If you are lucky, there may be a short history of the library service prepared as a thesis or for an anniversary celebration. Programmes of opening ceremonies sometimes also include a potted history of the library service up to that point. It hardly needs me to say that thesis material is copyright, but I am constantly amazed at the cavalier attitude displayed by some people to the original unpublished work of others.

I now pass on to the short histories mentioned in the previous paragraph, which I have seen and consulted. They are as follows:

BATT, CHRISTOPHER
Lambeth Public Libraries, the First Ten Years (undated typescript).

COWELL, J.
The Background and History of the Public Library Movement in Marylebone before the creation of the Greater London Boroughs in 1965. (Thesis submitted for the M.A. degree, University of Loughborough 1970 [typescript].)

FINCHAM, HENRY WALTER
James Duff Brown and the Finsbury Libraries. Notes on a meeting with Henry Fincham in the 1950's when he was over 90. He was a Finsbury Library Commissioner (undated typescript).

GROSS, STELLA
The Bennett Collection of Stained and Painted Glass (in Hammersmith Central Library – undated typescript).

HASKER, L. F.
To Commemorate the Approaching Jubilee of Her Most Gracious Majesty. An Outline of the Evolution of the Fulham Public Libraries, 1887–1963 (typescript, 1963).

HEARNE, CHRISTINE K.
The History and Development of Hampstead Public Libraries (undated typescript, but post 1965).

HOWSON, JAMES
Mutual Improvement: the Early Years of Barking Library (undated typescript).

ISLINGTON PUBLIC LIBRARIES
(Golden Jubilee 1906–1956)
A Programme of Events in Libraries. (This was preceded by a short historical introduction, 1956.)

JONES, ARTHUR C.
Paddington Public Libraries – A Short History (typescript, 1965).

MARION, CHARLES
Paltry Plumstead: or the Bobbery about a Bob. Reprinted from the *Woolwich and Plumstead Echo*. A somewhat tedious tract about the adoption of the Public Libraries Acts in Plumstead (undated, but clearly Victorian).

MASSEY, H. G.
Kensington Libraries Service. A short historical introduction is included (typescript, 1950).

MITCHELL, MARGARET B.
A History of Kingston upon Thames Public Library, 1880–1904. Produced as part of the post-graduate diploma course at the College of Librarianship, Wales (typescript, 1971).

MURRAY, IAN, WOODMAN, W. H. and LEA, E. G.
Farewell to Wood Green. Notes on the Wood Green Library (typescript, 1973).

MYSON, W.
The Story of the Wimbledon Library Service (typescript, revised, 1966).

TURNER, FRED
The History and Antiquities of Brentford. Chapter XVII gives a long and interesting account of the Brentford Library Services (St. Georges Press, The Butts, Brentford, 1922).

WEST HAM PUBLIC LIBRARIES AND TECHNICAL INSTRUCTION COMMITTEE
A Souvenir Presented to J. Passmore Edwards. It includes an account of the West Ham Library Service by Alfred Cotgreave (West Ham Corporation, 1898).

WRIGHT, P. J.
Public Library Services, 1909–1969 (London Borough of Redbridge – typescript, 1969).

Also the Holborn and Hampstead Annual Reports of 1963/64 contains short historical sections and so does that of Ealing for the same year, entitled *Respice – Prospice, 1883–1964*. The City of Westminster is especially well documented with three works. These are two reports, one for 1949/50 and the other for 1962/64 and a separate publication entitled *Great Smith Street Public Library, 1857–1957*. All three contain a great deal of valuable historical material.

For the present student of architecture, the scene is an almost total blank. The Penguin *Buildings of England* series under the general editorship of Sir Nikolaus Pevsner, covers public libraries only haphazardly. The relevant volumes for Greater London are London 1, which deals with the Cities of London and Westminster (3rd edition, 1973), London 2 for the former Metropolitan Boroughs (1952), Middlesex (1951), Surrey (2nd edition, 1971), Essex (2nd edition, 1965) and West Kent and the Weald (1969). *The Survey of London* volumes (Survey Committee, L.C.C. and subsequently G.L.C.) have dealt so far with a relatively small part of Greater London and only Volume XXVI (St. Mary, Lambeth, Part 2 – Southern Area) with six Lambeth public libraries and the Upper Norwood Joint Library comes anywhere near a reasonable coverage.

Luckily, this imbalance is to some extent corrected by the professional architectural and local government press of the period up to the first world war, which contains a great deal of useful material. The relevant periodicals are the *Builder* (from 1842 onwards), *Building News* (1857–1926), the *Architectural Review* (from 1896 onwards), the *British Architect* (1874–1919), the *Architect* (1869–1893), *London* (1893–1898), the *Surveyor and Municipal & County Engineer* (1893–1962), the *Builders' Journal and Architectural Record* (1895–1910) and the *Municipal Journal* (from 1893 onwards).

However, the views naturally reflect the time when they were written and there is clearly a need for somebody to tackle the pre-1914 public library buildings of Greater London in a thorough and systematic fashion from the standpoint of the present time.

Index of Buildings Illustrated

Buildings in italics no longer exist. Buildings in normal type are still in use as libraries. Buildings preceded by one asterisk still exist, but are no longer used for library purposes. The names in brackets are those of the relevant, post 1965, London Boroughs.

Balham (Wandsworth)
  Ramsden Road 87
Battersea (Wandsworth)
  Central 72
  Lurline Gardens 87
Brentford (Hounslow)
  Central 48
Camberwell (Southwark)
  Dulwich 62
  * Livesey 79
Chelsea (Kensington & Chelsea)
  Central 41
  Queens Park 58
Chiswick (Hounslow)
  Central 26
City of London (City of London)
  * Guildhall Library 81, 82, 91, 96
Clerkenwell *see* Finsbury
Croydon (Croydon)
  Central 59
Cubitt Town *see* Poplar
Deptford (Lewisham)
  New Cross 76
Dulwich *see* Camberwell
Ealing (Ealing)
  Central 24
East Ham (Newham)
  The Limes 30
  Manor Park 40, 65
  North Woolwich 30
Edmonton (Enfield)
  Central 36, 63
Eltham *see* Woolwich
Erith (Bexley)
  Central 73, 75
Finsbury (Islington)
  Central 59, 75, 77, 80
Guildhall *see* City of London
Hackney (Hackney)
  Central 45, 71
Haggerston *see* Shoreditch
Hammersmith (Hammersmith)
  Central 30, 44, 69, 74, 78, 95
  Shepherd's Bush 33, 99

Hampstead (Camden)
  * Central 41, 60, 83
  Belsize 42, 70
Highmans Park *see* Walthamstow
Ilford (Redbridge)
  Seven Kings 68
Islington (Islington)
  Central 69
  Central (unsuccessful plan) 70
Kensington (Kensington & Chelsea)
  North Kensington 67, 74
  * Vestry Hall/Central Library 27, 86
Kingston upon Thames (Kingston upon Thames)
  Central 50, 61
  Clattern House 26
Lambeth (Lambeth)
  Central 46
  Minet 64, 74
  South Lambeth 64
Lewisham (Lewisham)
  Manor House 25
Leyton (Waltham Forest)
  Town Hall/Library 27
Manor Park *see* East Ham
New Cross *see* Deptford
Paddington (Westminster)
  Queens Park 58
Penge (Bromley)
  Oakfield Road 25
Petersham (Richmond upon Thames)
  * Farm Lodge (private residence) 11
Plumstead *see* Woolwich
Poplar (Tower Hamlets)
  Brunswick Road 66, 79
  Cubitt Town 29
Putney (Wandsworth)
  Disraeli Road 86, 101, 102
Rotherhithe (Southwark)
  Town Hall/Library 28
  120 Lower Road 28
St. George's in the East *see* Stepney
St. Pancras (Camden)
  Central Libraries (proposed) 15, 71
Seven Kings *see* Ilford

Shepherd's Bush *see* Hammersmith
Shoreditch (Hackney)
  * Haggerston 63
Southwark (Southwark)
  Central 81
Stepney (Tower Hamlets)
  St. George's in the East 63, 80
  Whitechapel 62
Stoke Newington (Hackney)
  Central 70, 77, 87
Teddington (Richmond upon Thames)
  Waldegrave Road 75
Tottenham (Haringey)
  Central 64
  * The Chestnuts 26
  Eaton House 29
Twickenham (Richmond upon Thames)
  Central 43
Wandsworth (Wandsworth)
  West Hill 64, 87
Walthamstow (Waltham Forest)
  Central 54, 74, 77, 79, 87, 106
  Highams Park 31
  Rosebank 31, 54
West Ham (Newham)
  Central 38, 39, 52, 83, 101
  Rokeby House 31
Westminster (Westminster)
  City of Westminster Literary, Scientific & Mechanics' Institution frontispiece – as adapted to *Great Smith Street Branch* 23
  Queens Park 58
  * St. Martins 37, 51
  Victoria (Buckingham Palace Road) 68, 78, 81, 86
Whitechapel *see* Stepney
Wimbledon (Merton)
  Central 61, 95, 100
Wood Green (Haringey)
  Central 55
  * Earlham Grove House 27
Woolwich (Greenwich)
  Central 68, 82
  Eltham 63
  Plumstead 84